Botany

Disclaimer

Adult supervision is required when working on these projects. No responsibility is implied or taken for anyone who sustains injuries as a result of using the materials or ideas or performing the procedures put forth in this book. Use proper laboratory equipment such as gloves, safety glasses, and protective clothing, and take other safety precautions such as tying up loose hair and clothing, and washing your hands when the work is done.

Use chemicals, dry ice, boiling water, or any heating element with extra care. Hazardous chemicals and cultures must be handled and disposed of according to appropriate directions set forth by your sponsor. Follow your science fair's rules and regulations and/or standard scientific practices and procedures as set forth by your school or other governing body.

Additional safety precautions and warnings are mentioned throughout the text. If you use common sense and make safety your first consideration, you will create a safe, fun, educational, and rewarding project.

Botany

High-School Science Fair Experiments

H. Steven Dashefsky

TAB Books

Division of McGraw-Hill, Inc.

New York San Francisco Washington, D.C. Auckland Bogotá
Caracas Lisbon London Madrid Mexico City Milan
Montreal New Delhi San Juan Singapore
Sydney Tokyo Toronto

©1995 by **TAB Books**.
Published by TAB Books, a division of McGraw-Hill, Inc.

pbk   1 2 3 4 5 6 7 8 9 DOC/DOC 9 9 8 7 6 5 4
hc   1 2 3 4 5 6 7 8 9 DOC/DOC 9 9 8 7 6 5 4

Library of Congress Cataloging-in-Publication Data
Dashefsky, H. Steve
    Botany : high-school science fair projects / by H. Steven
Dashefsky.
      p.   cm.
    Includes index
    ISBN 0-07-015684-0   ISBN 0-07-015685-9
    1. Botany projects. I. Title.
QK52.6.D37   1994
581'.078—dc20
                                           94-34890
                                           CIP

Acquisitions editor: Kim Tabor
Editorial team: Joanne Slike, Executive Editor
                Lori Flaherty, Managing Editor
                Michilinda Kindsey, Book Editor
                Daniel J. Blaustein, Technical Reviewer
                Joann Woy, Indexer
Production team: Katherine G. Brown, Director
                Ollie Harmon, Coding
                Susan E. Hansford, Coding
                Brenda Wilhide, Computer Artist
                Wanda S. Ditch, Desktop Operator
                Nancy K. Mickley, Proofreading   GEN1
Designer: Jaclyn J. Boone   0156859

Acknowledgments

Many of the experiments in this book were adapted from original International Science and Engineering Fair (ISEF) projects. I want to thank the following young scientists for their outstanding projects and wish them the best of luck in their future scientific endeavors. All of these projects were edited and, in some cases, modified for use in this book.

- Pooja Sawhney (Bishop Fenwick High School, Massachusetts) for using Natural Pesticides, Project 1.
- Emily Raybuck for Natural Fertilizers, Project 2.
- Lara Tobin for Hydroponics, Project 3.
- Johanna Hopkinson for De-icing Road Salts, Project 4.
- Matthew Adkins for Artificial Coral Reefs, Project 5.
- Melissa Lynn Jones (Zion Chapel High School, Alabama) for Distilled Saltwater, Project 6.
- Ryan Viator for Compost as a Fertilizer, Project 7.
- Marcia Sajewicz for Acid Rain and Direct Contact, Project 8.
- Philip Berthelsen for Electromagnetic Radiation and Algae, Project 9.
- Jennifer Ellis for The Origins of Acid Rain, Project 10.
- Ariel Frometa (Everett High School, Massachusetts), for Holes/in the Ozone and/Unicellular Organisms, Project 11.
- Justin Magnifico for Detergents and Plant Growth, Project 12.
- Sarah Greer for The Hole in the Ozone and /Terrestrial Plants, Project 13.
- Amanda Boehmer for Indoor Air Pollution and Houseplants, Project 14.
- Bernadette Quirk (Brockton High School, Massachusetts), for Dried-Up Ponds, Project 15.
- Carla Suarez-Soto (Immaculate Conception School Academy, Puerto Rico) for Using Algae for Medicinal Purposes, Project 16.
- Megan Bronson for Plant Growth Regulators, Project 18.
- Julie Gillespie (Burkburnett High School, Texas), for Ethylene Gas and Plant Growth, Project 19.

Contents

Part 4
Plants and Plant Life

Safety and supervision

All of the projects in this book require an adult sponsor to ensure the student's safety and the safety of others. Science Service, Inc. is an organization that sets science fair rules, regulations, and safety guidelines and holds the International Science and Engineering Fairs (ISEF). This book recommends and assumes that students performing projects from this book follow ISEF guidelines as they pertain to adult supervision. ISEF guidelines state that students undertaking science fair projects must have adult sponsors assigned to them.

The adult sponsor is described as a teacher, parent, professor, or scientist in whose lab the student is working. For the purpose of this book, the sponsor will usually be the student's teacher. The sponsor must have a solid background in science and be in close contact with the student throughout the project. The adult sponsor is responsible for the safety of the student while conducting the research, including the handling of all equipment, chemicals, and organisms.

The sponsor must also be familiar with the regulations and commonly approved practices that govern chemical and equipment usage, experimental techniques, the use of laboratory animals, cultures and microorganisms, and proper disposal techniques.

If the adult sponsor is not qualified to handle all of these responsibilities, the sponsor must assign other adults who can fulfill these responsibilities. Most science fairs require appropriate forms, which identify the adult sponsor and his or her qualifications, be filled out before proceeding with a project.

The sponsor is responsible for reviewing the student's research plan and ensuring the experimentation is done within local, federal, and ISEF (or other appropriate governing body) guidelines.

The entire project should be read and reviewed by the student and the adult sponsor before beginning. The sponsor should determine which portions of the experiment the student can perform without supervision and which portions will require supervision. In addition, ⚠ symbols throughout the text indicate where extra caution, such as wearing safety goggles and gloves, must be taken.

For a copy of the ISEF's rules and regulations, contact Science Service, Inc. at 1719 N Street, N.W., Washington, D.C. 20036, (202) 785-2255. The ISEF booklet includes a checklist for the adult sponsor, approval forms, and valuable information on all aspects of participating in a science fair. Everyone should have this information before competing in a science fair.

How to use this book

There are two ways to use this book. If you are new to science fair projects and feel that you need a great deal of technical guidance, you can use the projects as explained in this book with few if any adjustments. The projects are good, solid, and, in many cases, award-winning science fair projects. However, don't be afraid to use these projects as models to mold into your own form.

This book provides core experiments with many suggestions to encourage you to expand the scope or adjust the focus of each experiment. Your sponsor can help you modify these projects. Suggestions are given in the "Going further" and "Suggested research" sections of each project to help you modify the experiment.

Each project has the following sections: a) Background, b) Project overview, c) Materials list, d) Procedures, e) Analysis, f) Going further, and g) Suggested research.

Background

The Background section provides basic information about the topic. It offers you a frame of reference so you can see the importance of the topic and why research is necessary to advance our understanding of the topic. This section can be considered the initial step in your literature search. (See the next section for more about your literature search.) Reading the project Background will help you know whether the subject sparks your interest.

Project overview

If the Background section interests you, continue reading. The Project overview describes the purpose of the project. It explains the problems that exist and poses questions that the experiment is intended to answer. These questions can be used to formulate your hypothesis. Be sure to discuss this section, as well as the next, with your sponsor to see if the requirements imposed can realistically be met.

Materials list

The Materials list section details everything needed to perform the experiment. Be sure you have access to everything before beginning. Some equipment or apparatus is expensive. Check with your sponsor to see if all the equipment is available in your school or can be borrowed elsewhere. Be sure your budget can handle necessary purchases. A list of scientific supply houses is provided in the Sources at the back of the book.

Although most of us don't think of research scientists as hammer-and-nails people, they must be. Building a device or experimental workstation often involves many trips to the hardware store for supplies, a little sweat on the brow, and a lot of ingenuity.

Living plants can be ordered from scientific supply houses or, in many cases, purchased from local garden centers. Organisms such as bacterial cultures must be ordered from the supply houses. Others, such as insects, can be ordered, purchased locally, or caught depending on the project, your location, and the time of year.

If you are using live organisms, work with your sponsor to be sure you adhere to all science fair regulations and standard biological research practices. Before beginning, discuss with your sponsor the proper way to dispose of any hazardous materials, chemicals, or cultures.

Procedures

The Procedures section provides step-by-step instructions to perform the experiment and suggestions on how to collect data. Read through this section with your sponsor before undertaking the project. Illustrations are often used to clarify procedures.

Analysis

The Analysis section doesn't draw conclusions for you. Instead, it asks questions to help you analyze and interpret the data so you can come to your own conclusions. In many cases, empty tables and charts are provided for you to begin your data collection. You should convert as much of your raw data as possible into line and bar graphs and/or pie charts.

Some experiments might require statistical analysis to determine if there are significant differences between the experimental group and the control group. Check with your sponsor to see if you should perform statistical analysis for your project and if so, what type. See the Further reading section for books that can help you analyze your data.

Going further

Going further is a vital part of every project. It lists ways to continue researching the topic beyond the original experiment. These suggestions can be followed as is or, even more importantly, they might inspire you to think of a new twist or angle to take while performing the project. These suggestions might show ways to more thoroughly cover the subject matter and/or show you how to broaden the scope of the project.

The best way to ensure an interesting and fully developed project is to include one or more of the suggestions from the Going further section or include an idea of your own that was inspired by this section.

Suggested research

The Suggested research section suggests new directions to follow while researching the project. It often suggests material to read and organizations, companies, or other sources to contact. Using these additional resources might turn your project into a winner.

Part 1

Before You Begin

Before delving into any scientific experiment, there are three things to understand: the terminology used, the methodology required, and the suitability of the project to your own situation and preferences. The following three chapters examine these elements.

1

An introduction to botany

Botany is the science of plants and plant life. It is a very broad science that studies plants of all shapes and sizes ranging from microscopic organisms, such as some algae, to enormous specimens, such as the Giant Sequoia.

Botanists are interested in everything from the structure of plant cells to the geographic distribution of certain plants and the effect of acid rain on forests or pond life. Because botany covers such a wide range of topics, it can be divided into numerous subdisciplines. Some examples are: plant cytology (plant cells), plant ecology, plant embryology (development), plant morphology (structure), plant taxonomy (classification), ethnobotany (plants' influence on human culture), and paleobotany (fossilized plants).

Botany can also be divided by the different types of plants scientists are interested in studying. For example, *algology* is the study of algae, *bryology* is the study of mosses, and *agrostology* is the study of grasses.

Furthermore, botany is the foundation of many applied sciences, including agronomy (soil science), forestry, floriculture, horticulture, and landscape architecture.

What separates plants from animals?

Roughly 1.5 million types of organisms have been identified on our planet and approximately half a million of them are plants. But what exactly is a plant? Plants are *autotrophs*, meaning they produce their own food by converting sunlight, or radiant energy, directly into chem-

3

ical energy during the process of *photosynthesis*. Plants contain the compound *chlorophyll*, which is responsible for photosynthesis. The fact that plants contain chlorophyll and are capable of photosynthesis is the primary difference between plants and animals. Because animals cannot produce their own food, they are called *heterotrophs*, meaning they must consume their food by eating plants or other animals.

Another important difference between plants and animals is their cell walls. In an advanced plant, a cell wall surrounds the living part of each cell. This wall is rigid and often provides support to the organism. It usually consists of cellulose and does not allow materials to pass through. Animals, on the other hand, have very thin cell membranes with no walls surrounding the cells. The cell membrane in an animal does not provide any support to the organism and it is *permeable*, meaning certain materials can pass through it.

There are other differences as well. Plants cannot move about freely as do animals. Almost all animals have nervous systems of some sort that allow them to react rapidly to stimuli such as an attack from a predator. Plants do not have nervous systems, so they respond to stimuli very slowly compared to animals.

Classifying plants

Scientists classify all forms of life according to how closely related they are to one another. You can compare this classification system to a file cabinet that contains many drawers, and each drawer contains many folders and dividers. Each organism is on its own sheet of paper and placed somewhere in this file cabinet.

The more closely related two types of plants are, the more closely their sheets of paper are placed in the cabinet. For example, a moss and a pine tree would be placed in two different drawers because they are so different. However, a pine tree and a spruce tree would appear not only in the same drawer, but within the same folder because they are so similar.

To expand this comparison, imagine there are two file cabinets; one cabinet is labelled "Plants," and the other "Animals." Each cabinet represents a *kingdom*. Let's concentrate on the plant cabinet. Imagine five drawers in this cabinet. Each drawer represents a phylum. Each phylum contains plants that have certain characteristics in common. Dandelions and white pine are found in the drawer labelled "Tracheophyta" because they both have vascular tissues divided into roots, stems, and leaves. Mosses and liverworts are found in the drawer labelled "Bryophyta" because they don't have vascular tissues.

Inside each drawer is a series of folders. These folders represent *classes* of organisms that have even more similar characteristics. For example, our dandelion and white pine both go into the same drawer, phylum "Tracheophyta," but go into different folders (classes) within the drawer. The dandelion is placed in a folder labelled class "Angiospermae," which contains plants with flowers. The white pine is placed a folder labelled "Gymnospermae" because it has seeds with no flowers.

The classification system continues to distinguish which plants are most closely related to each other by placing them in orders, families, genera, and species. *Species* represents the most specific group of plants. In our example, the species is the sheet of paper containing the scientific name of the plant.

Some of the folders are thicker than others because some contain many more species. For example, the folder labelled "Angiospermae" is enormous because it holds approximately 235,000 species, while the folder labelled "Coniferinae" only holds about 550 species (see Fig. 1-1). Research which file cabinet, drawer, folder, and dividers would contain the sheets of paper containing a dandelion, white pine, moss growing on a rock, and algae growing on the surface of a stagnant pond.

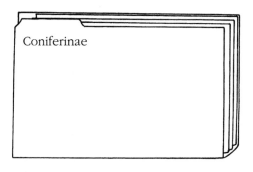

Coniferinae

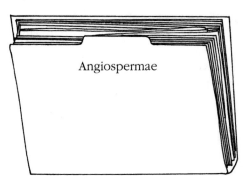

Angiospermae

1-1
Some folders (classes) are very thick because they contain numerous species, while others are very thin because they contain far fewer species.

There are many different classification systems; some have three kingdoms, some four, and some five. The most accepted system today uses five kingdoms. In this system, the plant kingdom contains only multicellular plants. Single-celled organisms, such as *Euglena* and *Amoeba*, are placed in the kingdom Protista. There are animal-like protists and plantlike protists. Plantlike protists are *autotrophic*, meaning they contain chlorophyll and are capable of photosynthesis. The projects in this book encompass a broad definition of "plant," including all organisms capable of photosynthesis, from single-celled protists to large seaweeds, flowers, and trees.

Thus, the experiments in this book include organisms found in two kingdoms, Protista and Plantae. Some of these projects are about green algae, which are in the kingdom Protista, Chlorophyta phylum, and about the euglenoids, which are in the Euglenophyta phylum. There are experiments about many types of plants in the kingdom Plantae, Tracheophyta (vascular plants) phylum, and class Angiospermae (flowering plants).

Parts of plants

Most of the projects in this book deal with the largest and best known of the plants—the flowering plants. These plants have four basic parts: roots, stems, leaves and flowers, plus a vascular system.

Roots

Roots play two major roles: they anchor the plant firmly in the soil, and they collect water and minerals from the soil and deliver them to the stem. There are two basic types of flowering plants, each with a different type of root. Most of the *dicots* (plants with two *cotyledons*, or seed leaves) have *taproots*—large, thick roots that reach deep into the earth. These roots store food for periods of dormancy, like winter (see Fig. 1-2).

Most of the *monocots* (plants with one cotyledon) have fibrous roots, which are composed of numerous, thin filaments that remain near the surface of the soil.

Some monocots and dicots have a third and unusual type of root called *adventitious roots*. These roots are used by climbing plants such as ivy to help the plant hold on.

Stems

A plant's above-ground shoot, called the stem, supports the leaves and flowers. The stem contains a vascular system, which transports

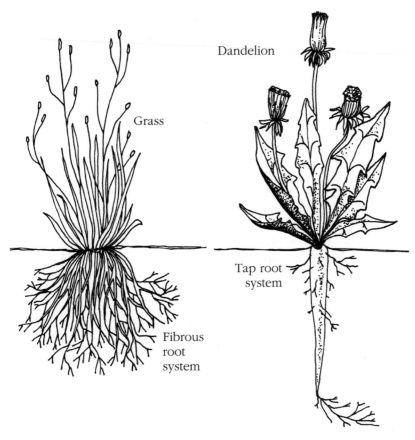

Dandelion

Grass

Tap root
system

Fibrous
root
system

1-2 *Some plants grow long tap roots, while others grow fibrous roots.*

fluids throughout the plant just as our circulatory systems carry blood throughout our bodies.

There are many types of stems. They can be straight or branched, upright, creeping, or climbing. There are also many highly specialized types of stems, such as those that form bulbs, tubers, and rhizomes, which are all underground food storage organs.

Plants are either *woody* or *herbaceous*. Long-lived, large plants have more woody material than short-lived, smaller plants. The woody material is actually a substance called *lignin*. The more lignin that is present, the heavier and stronger the stem and the more weight it can support. Tree stems contain large amounts of lignin while grasses have small amounts of lignin.

Leaves

Photosynthesis occurs primarily in a plant's leaves, although it can occur elsewhere. Most leaves are flat and broad in shape and are therefore called *blades*. Blades bend and twist to present the greatest surface area to the sun. Leaves usually get smaller toward the top of a plant so they don't block sunlight from the leaves below.

Leaves can be arranged in an alternate, opposite, or whorled fashion as seen in Fig. 1-3. Leaves are also either *simple*, meaning there is only one blade, or *compound*, meaning there are many blades or leaflets, as seen in Fig. 1-4.

Because leaves are responsible for photosynthesis, they must have a method of allowing carbon dioxide in and oxygen out. Leaves have many microscopic openings called *stomata*, on the underside to allow these gases to pass in and out. The stomata are opened and closed by *guard cells*, specialized cells which surround the openings. Some plants have stomata on both sides of the leaves and the stems as well.

Flowers

Flowers are the reproductive structures of flowering plants, responsible for producing the seeds that will continue the species into another generation. Flowers are composed of modified shoots and leaves.

A typical flower consists of a male structure called the *stamen*, which is composed of anthers and filaments. This is where pollen is produced. The female part of the flower, called the *pistil*, is composed of the stigma style and ovary. After the stigma receives pollen, the seed develops in the ovary.

Vascular systems

The roots and stem contain a series of tubes, called the vascular system, which transports material throughout the plant. These tubes consist of *xylem* and *phloem*. The xylem transports water and dissolved minerals upward from the roots to the rest of the plant. The phloem moves material up and down through the plant, primarily transporting compounds that were synthesized by the plant, such as carbohydrates from the leaves where they were made to the roots where they are stored.

Photosynthesis

As mentioned earlier, the most important distinguishing feature of a plant is its ability to create its own food. Through photosynthesis,

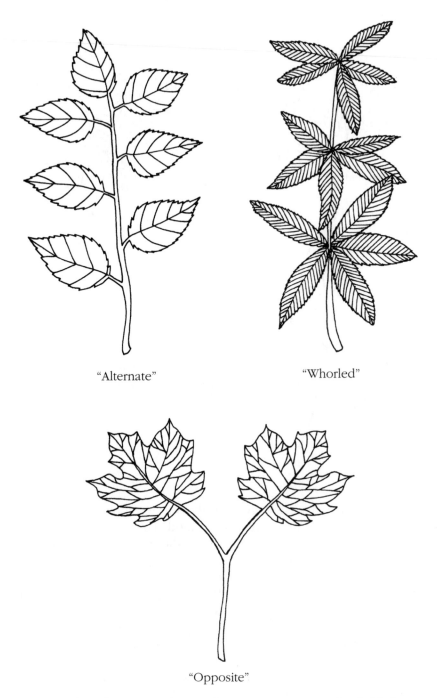

"Alternate"   "Whorled"

"Opposite"

1-3 *Leaves can be arranged in an alternate, opposite, or whorled fashion.*

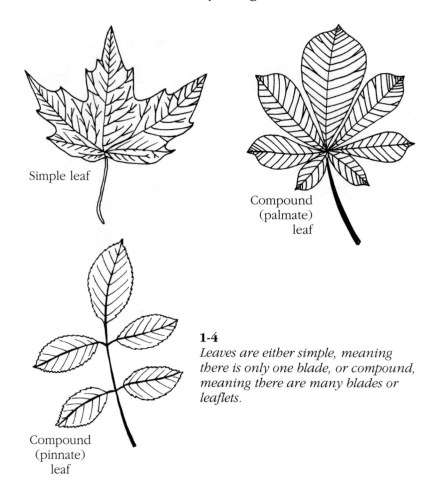

Simple leaf

Compound
(palmate)
leaf

1-4
*Leaves are either simple, meaning
there is only one blade, or compound,
meaning there are many blades or
leaflets.*

Compound
(pinnate)
leaf

plants convert radiant energy from the sun to stored, chemical energy—what we commonly refer to as food. This process occurs in a green pigment called chlorophyll with the assistance of many enzymes, which help make the biochemical reactions occur.

We know that the sun provides the energy needed to make this transformation occur, but what is the source of the chemicals needed? Carbon dioxide from the air and water from the soil provide the building blocks. These building blocks are used to create a simple sugar called *glucose*. When we refer to stored chemical energy, we are discussing glucose.

The sun provides the energy to take carbon dioxide and build glucose, which contains the stored energy. But how does the plant use this stored energy? The same way we do: through the process of *respiration*. During respiration, plants and animals break down glucose to

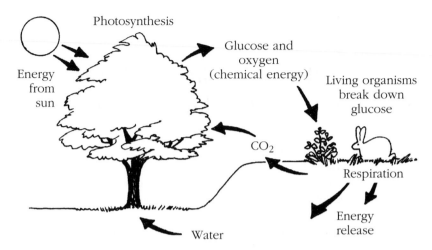

Photosynthesis

Glucose and
oxygen
(chemical energy)

Energy
from
sun

Living organisms
break down
glucose

CO_2

Respiration

Water

Energy
release

1-5 *Respiration allows plants to use the stored chemical energy that was produced during photosynthesis.*

release the energy stored within it, then use this energy to live (see Fig. 1-5).

Succession

As organisms live in their environment, they change that environment. As they change the environment, they usually make it less suitable for themselves and more favorable for other types of organisms. For example, in an open field you will find sun-loving plants growing at first. As these sun-loving plants grow, they shade the ground, making the field inhospitable to other sun-loving plants. However, shade-tolerant species will find the environment suitable. After some time, the shade-tolerant plants overtake the original sun-loving plants.

This is a simplified example of a process called *succession.* The first *community* (all the populations living in an area) to move into an area is called the *pioneer community.* Think of the first organisms to move into a recently abandoned farm or an area devastated by a fire or flood. The series of different communities that inhabit an area is called a *sere,* and the final community is called the *climax community.* The climax community is the final, stable community that shows little change. The entire process of succession can take 100 years or thousands of years, depending on the condition of the original habitat.

Understanding succession is important when studying plants because it explains a great deal about why plants inhabit an area when they do. When studying plants in the field, it is useful to understand the typical succession found in that environment.

Studying, collecting, and photographing plants in the field

Some of the projects in this book involve studying or collecting plants in the field. Even projects that are strictly lab-oriented can benefit from collections of samples or photographs of specimens in their natural habitats. People, including judges, like to have a frame of reference when reading about a plant, whether it be an algae mat growing on a pond or a pine growing in a forest.

Collections can include vials of plant parts, potted plants if small enough, pressed leaves, samples of bark or full-color photographs. Following are some pointers for the field botanist setting out to collect or photograph specimens.

Identification

The first thing you must be able to do is identify the plant you want to study. A good field guide is an invaluable tool. Be sure the guide has a *key*, a simple way of identifying plants. A key asks a series of questions; each question leads you to another until the questions stop and the key lists the name of the organism. The Sources section of this book gives the names of several good field guides and keys.

Identification equipment

Many of the questions asked in the key will require the use of a hand lens and probes. A hand lens, or magnifying glass, helps you see the small features of a plant. The lens need not be expensive, but should be capable of at least 8×. Larger lenses are easier to handle and less likely to get lost.

In many situations, it is necessary to dissect part of a plant. A fine forceps, which is a sort of tweezer, a probe like the one your dentist uses to clean your teeth, and a sharp hobby knife are usually all you'll need. Most of these tools should be available in your school lab or a science store.

Collecting plants

Plants can be collected for potting or to be dried and pressed. Whenever you collect plants or parts of plants, collect in a responsible manner. Be sure you have identified the plant in the field so you know you are not taking an endangered or threatened species. If only part of a plant is needed, use sharp pruning shears and seal the wounds with dressing if possible. If you are collecting only seeds, leave more than you take.

When collecting specimens, use a rigid rubber container with an airtight lid. Place the plant in the container, covered with paper. Multiple layers of paper and specimens can be placed in one container. Be sure to label each piece of paper and cross-reference it in your journal with pertinent information including specimen type, location, and date collected.

Displaying plants

Obviously, the best way to display plants is in their natural settings. This, of course, isn't practical in a science fair project because you are not going to get the judges to take a hike with you. If your specimen is a potted plant, such as a bean or tomato plant, you could display the entire live plant if the fair allows live organisms. Your best alternatives are to either take full-color photographs or display dry, preserved specimens. For complete details on ways to preserve your plant specimens and for information about photographing plants, refer to the Sources at the end of the book.

2

Scientific research

A science fair gives you the opportunity to not only learn about a topic, but to participate in the discovery process. You probably won't discover something previously unknown to humankind (although you never can tell), but you will perform the process through which discoveries are made. Advances in science move forward slowly, with each experiment building upon a previous one and preparing researchers to perform the next.

Advances in medicine, biotechnology, agriculture, and virtually all scientific disciplines proceed one step at a time. A typical science fair project allows you to see what it is like to take one or two of these steps for yourself. The following typifies how science marches on.

A problem such as whether compost can replace commercial fertilizers might be solved by a series of experiments. First, preliminary lab studies can determine the chemical composition of compost to see if the potential exists for compost to replace fertilizer. Lab tests could then be performed to see how much compost produces the same growth as a specified amount of commercial fertilizer.

Once an optimal amount of compost is identified, scientists begin small field testing to see if what works in the lab works in the garden. If favorable results are obtained from these experiments, large scale tests could begin on a research farm.

Any one of these experiments might result in negative results. For example, the compost tested might not have enough nutrients to completely replace the fertilizer. Even these studies are valuable, however, since they provide information that keeps scientists on the correct track.

The scientific method

As you saw in the previous example, each experiment was necessary before the next could be performed and the entire progression was necessary before a successful conclusion could be reached. Scientific research, no matter how simple or how sophisticated, must follow a protocol that demands consistency and, most importantly, duplicity. When one scientist or research team makes a discovery, others must verify it. The scientific method provides a framework for researchers to follow. It assures a highly focused, reproducible sequence of events.

The following descriptions enumerate the four steps in the scientific method and relate the steps to sections of this book.

Problem

First, you must formulate the question you want to answer or problem you would like to solve. For example, can distilled saltwater be used to grow hydroponic plants? Does acid rain harm algae? The Project overview section of each project in this book gives questions and problems to think about. The Going further and Suggested research sections might inspire you to think of additional problems.

Hypothesis

A hypothesis is an educated guess, based on library research, that offers a possible answer to the questions posed. You might hypothesize that distilled saltwater can be used to grow hydroponic plants or that acid rain does have a harmful effect on algae. Form a hypothesis to answer the questions in the Project overview section of each project.

Experimentation

The experiment is designed to determine whether the hypothesis is correct. If the hypothesis was incorrect, a well-designed experiment helps determine why.

First, you must design and set up the experiment. How must you prepare the experiment and what procedures must you follow to test the hypothesis? What materials are needed? What live organisms, if any, are needed? What step-by-step procedures must be followed during the experiment? What observations and data must be made and collected while the experiment is running? Once these questions have been answered, the actual experiment can begin.

During the actual experiment, make observations and collect data. Your results must be documented for study and analysis. The more details, the better. There are three important things to remember when conducting an experiment: take notes, take notes, and take notes. The most common mistake new scientists make is thinking they will remember small details. If you always carry a notebook and pencil when working on your project, this won't become a problem. Some science fairs require that you submit the project notebook along with a brief abstract of the project. Some fairs require or encourage a full-length report of the project as well. See the section on Science fair guidelines in chapter 3.

The Materials list section of each project lists all the materials needed for each experiment and the Procedures section provides step-by-step instructions. Suggestions are given on what observations should be made and what data should be collected.

Another aspect of experimentation is the importance of replication. For any project to be considered valid scientific work, the experimental groups should be replicated as many times as is practical. Multiple groups can then be averaged together or, better yet, statistically analyzed. For the projects in this book, try to perform all experimental groups in triplicate. Replication reduces that chances of collecting spurious data which will result in incorrect conclusions.

Analysis

After the experiment is complete, you must analyze the data and draw conclusions to determine if your hypothesis is correct. Create tables, charts, or graphs to help analyze the data. The Procedures section of each project suggests observations to make and data to collect while running the experiment. The Analysis section asks important questions to help you analyze the data and often contains empty tables or charts to fill in with your data. This book provides guidance, but you must draw your own conclusions.

Your conclusions should be based on your original hypothesis. Was it correct? If it was incorrect, what did you learn from the experiment? What new hypothesis can you create and test? Something is always learned while performing an experiment, even if it's how not to perform the next experiment.

Building on past projects

Just as scientists advance the work of other scientists, so too can you advance the work of those who have performed science fair projects before you. Rather than copying their work exactly, try to think of the next logical step to take in that line of research. Possibly you can put a new twist on a previous experiment. If acid rain can damage algae, can it harm flowering plants? Or, if the original experiment was performed *in vitro* (in a test tube), can you perform a similar experiment *in vivo* (in nature)?

Abstracts of previous science fair projects are available from the Science Service in Washington D.C. See the Reference section in this book for this and other sources of successful science fair projects. Also see the Selecting a project section of this book for more on this topic.

3

Choosing a project

The best way to select a project is find out what interests you. Did you ever wonder which plants best help clean the air in your home? Or whether de-icing road salts applied during the winter are harmful to plants? Have you considered the effects of acid rain, ultra-violet radiation, or electromagnetic radiation on plants? Do you ponder the medicinal qualities of garlic or think about the saying, "One rotten apple spoils the whole barrel"? If so, you have only to narrow the field and select a project that not only interests you, but inspires you to learn more.

If, however, you are unsure of where your interest lies, try one or more of the following lines of investigation. Once a subject sparks your imagination or sets you wondering, you should be able to select a project with relative ease.

This book contains 20 science fair projects about plants. Look through the Table of Contents for topics to research. Read through the Background and Project overview sections of each project. Every project in this book can be adjusted, expanded upon, or fine tuned in some way to personalize your investigation.

After reading through these sections, think about how you can put your own signature on the experimentation. The Going further and Suggested research sections are designed to help you personalize each project. If you find yourself saying, "I'd like to know more about..." something you see, you're well on your way to selecting a project about plants. Speak with your sponsor for suggestions.

Take a botanical tour

What better way to expand your botanical horizons than to see what is growing around you? Begin by looking around your home, school, and town. Look not only at the plants that were placed there on purpose, but those that are growing wild. Look in abandoned fields, wooded areas, hiking trails, and nature preserves. You don't have to live in the country to find plenty of interesting plants. Urban botany is the study of plants that live in cities. Look at the plants in a vacant lot or coming up through the cracks in a parking lot. Look along old railroad tracks, at sidewalks, and in small puddles.

If you have a lawn, investigate it. Is anything growing besides grass? Look for mosses in the grass and lichens on the trees. Why are they there? If you live on or near a farm, investigate it thoroughly. What other than the crop is growing? Look in open meadows, fields, and woodlots. If you live by the shore, look for shoreline plant life, which is unique. The possible places to look for plant life are as limitless as the possible topics for science fair projects.

Other sources

You've identified your areas of interest but still need more insight. Consider branching out by looking through science sections of newspapers such as the *New York Times*. Do you see articles about endangered species of plants or a new environmentally safe fertilizer?

Look at magazines such as *Popular Science, Discover* or *Omni*. Check the *Reader's Guide to Periodical Literature*, which is an index that lists articles in numerous magazines and gives brief synopses. Your school text books might also be helpful. Check references to other books, usually found at the end of each chapter.

Other sources that can help include educational television shows such as "NOVA," National Geographic specials, "Nature," and many others. Almost all of these shows are found on public television—check your local listings.

Talk to specialists in the field

Once you have a good idea for a project, consider talking with a professional. For example, if your project involves selecting the best house plants to clean the air, speak with a typical homeowner who has house plants, a botany professor at a nearby college, and the owner of a greenhouse who sells house plants.

Interesting science fair projects don't only involve equipment, chemicals, and cultures, but also what people have to say about the topic—pro, con, and indifferent.

Also, be sure to use any resources that are readily available. If you live near a small organic farm, large mechanized farm, water treatment plant, landfill, agricultural research station, or almost any type of facility that can contribute to your project, try to use it to your advantage. If you have a parent or friend who is involved in a business or profession applicable to your project, try to incorporate him or her into your research.

Put your signature on the project

All the projects in this book are good candidates for science fair projects. Putting your signature on one of these projects could make it an outstanding example of research. For instance, try to include portions of the Going further section, or delve into the Suggested research section. Ask a teacher, scientist, or business person to help you with an aspect of the research to make it truly unique and your own.

Before you begin

Before beginning a project, review the entire project with your sponsor to anticipate problems that might arise. Some projects must be done at a certain time of year. Some can be done in a day or two, while others can take a few weeks, months, or even longer.

Some projects use materials that are found around the home, but many require equipment or supplies that must be purchased from a local hardware store, science/nature store, or a scientific supply house. Your sponsor might have access to the organisms needed for the project. Plants such as mosses might be collected in the wild, bought at a garden center, or ordered from a scientific supply house.

Also, plan ahead financially. Look through the Materials List section of the experiment you choose. Be sure to budget materials you need for additions or modifications you made to the original project. Determine how and where you will get everything and how much it will cost. If you need live plants, can you collect them, get them from your sponsor or a nearby university, or must you purchase them? How much will it cost? Don't begin a project unless you can budget the appropriate amount of time and money as suggested by your sponsor.

Performing the experiment

Once you have selected a project, located your equipment, and budgeted expenses, you'll probably feel ready to begin. Before you tie on your lab coat, however, consider the following organizational and procedural suggestions.

Scheduling

It is a good idea to develop a schedule to assure you have a complete project in time for the fair. Have your sponsor approve your timetable. Leave yourself time to acquire the equipment, supplies, and organisms. Also, consider growing time. Some experiments involving plants take longer than those about other subjects because of the growth period involved.

Most science fair projects require a few months from start to finish if they are to be accomplished thoroughly. In many instances they can, and must, be completed in less time. It would be difficult to produce a prize-winning project, however, without plenty of time. Here is a general list of things to do that you should think about when preparing a timetable.

- Identify your adult sponsor.
- Choose a general topic.
- Establish a project notebook.
- List resources, including libraries, people, businesses, organizations, agencies, etc.
- Select reading materials and use bibliographies for more resources; begin a formal literature search.
- Select the exact project and develop a hypothesis.
- Write a detailed research plan and discuss it with your adult sponsor; have your sponsor sign off on the final research plan.
- Procure equipment, supplies, plants and other organisms, and all other materials.
- Follow up on your resource list: speak with experts, make all contacts, etc.
- Set up and begin experimentation.
- Collect data and rigorously take notes.
- Plan your exhibit display.
- Analyze data and draw conclusions.
- Write reports and have your sponsor review them.
- Write your final report and/or abstract. Make sure your notebook is available and legible.
- Complete and construct a dry run of exhibit display.
- Prepare for questions about your project.
- Disassemble and pack project for transport to fair.
- When the date of the fair arrives, set up your display, relax, and enjoy yourself.

The literature search

As you can see from the "to do" list, one of your first tasks is a litera- ture search of the problem you intend to study. Performing a literature search (library research) means reading everything you can get your hands on about your topic. Read newspapers, magazines, books, ab- stracts—anything related to the specific topic you are studying. Use online databases if available. Talk to as many people as possible who have some insight into your topic. Listen to the news on radio and television. As a result of your literature search, you might want to nar- row down or even change the exact problem you plan to study.

Once your literature search is complete and you have organized the data both on paper and in your mind, you should know exactly what problem you intend to study and be able to formulate a hypothesis.

The research plan

A research plan should be completed. You can use portions of this book to start your research plan, but you must go into additional de- tail and include all modifications. Before beginning the project, go through the research plan in detail with your adult sponsor to be sure your project is safe, attainable, suitable, and practical.

In many science fairs, the sponsor is required to sign off on the research plan, attesting that it has been reviewed and approved. It is important to review your particular fair's regulations so your project won't run into problems as you proceed.

Science fair guidelines

Almost all science fairs have formal guidelines or rules. Discuss with your sponsor the rules of your fair. For example, there might be a limit to the amount of money that can be spent on a project or cer- tain organisms might be prohibited. Review these guidelines and check that the experiment poses no conflicts.

Many science fairs require four basic components for all entries: 1) The actual notebook, used throughout the project, that contains data collection notes. Remember when taking your notes that they may be read by fair officials. If the notebook is also used as a field book, keep it dry and in good condition. Leaving it outside in one good downpour could sink your project. 2) An abstract of the project that briefly states the problem, proposed hypothesis, generalized pro- cedures, data collection methods, and conclusions. This is usually no more than 250 words long. 3) A full-length research paper. 4) The ex- hibition display.

The research paper

A research paper might be required by your fair, but consider writing one even if it isn't necessary. The experience of organizing a paper will serve you well in the future.

The research paper should include seven sections: 1) title page; 2) table of contents; 3) introduction; 4) procedures; 5) comprehensive discussion section explaining what you did and what went through your mind while performing the research and experimentation; 6) a separate conclusion that summarizes your results; and 7) a reference and credit section in which you list your sources and give credit to people, companies, organizations, or agencies who helped you. In the Sources section of this book is a list of books that detail how to write a research report.

The display

The exhibit display should be as informative as possible. Keep in mind that most people, including the judges, will only spend a short time looking at each presentation. Try to create a display that gets as much information across with the least amount of words as quickly as possible. Use graphs, charts, or tables to illustrate data. As the old saying goes, "A picture is worth a thousand words."

A display about plants is highlighted nicely by either photographs of your specimens or dry, preserved samples. Include photos or preserved specimens of not only the subjects or parts of subjects involved in the project, but also the plant in its natural setting. For example, if you are studying the bark of a Giant Redwood, have a sample of the bark and a photo of the actual tree.

Discuss with your sponsor any exhibit requirements such as special equipment, electrical outlets, and wiring needs. Live organisms, including microbial cultures of any type, are usually prohibited from display. Often, preserved specimens are also prohibited. At some fairs, no foods, wastes, or even water are allowed in an exhibit. Also, no flames, gases, or harmful chemicals are allowed. Find out what you can and cannot do before proceeding.

Many fairs have specific size requirements for the actual display and its backboard. For more information on building an exhibit display, see the "Further reading" section at the end of this book.

Judging

When beginning your project, keep in mind that adherence to the scientific method and attention to detail are crucial to the success of any project. Judges usually want to see a well-thought-out project and a knowledgeable individual who understands all aspects of his or her project.

Most science fairs assign a point value to various aspects of a project. For example, the research paper might be worth 30 points while the actual display might be worth 10 points. Request any information that might give you insight about the judgment criteria at your fair. This information can help you allocate your time and resources where they are most needed.

Part 2

Looking for Solutions

The projects in this section help you look for solutions to environmental problems associated with plants. Chapters 4, 5, and 10 are about using natural fertilizers such as compost instead of synthetic commercial fertilizers.

Chapters 6 and 9 investigate the use of water to grow plants. Chapter 6 studies water temperature and its effect on hydroponics, and Chapter 9 looks into the use of distilled water for plant growth.

Chapters 7 and 8 look at unique problems and solutions. Chapter 7 investigates alternatives to harmful road salts, and Chapter 8 studies the materials used to build artificial coral reefs.

4

Using natural pesticides

Can citrus oil, garlic, or jalapeño control insect pests?

Background

The use of commercial pesticides started 40 years ago as what was thought to be the solution to all our pest problems. Unfortunately, pesticides have come to haunt us. Though we apply far more pesticides today than we did 10 years ago, we lose more of our crops to pests. Why? Pests have become resistant to the pesticides. Thus, we use more pesticide but kill fewer pests.

The term *pesticide* is really a misnomer, since the word makes it sound as if only pests are killed, though most kill a broad spectrum of organisms. Rachel Carson, in her famous book, *Silent Spring*, suggested using the term *biocide* instead of *pesticide*, to reflect the fact that all life is jeopardized by pesticides, not just the pests.

How can we control and reduce pest damage without destroying other plants and animals? The perfect pesticide would achieve complete control of the targeted pest and be biodegradable and nontoxic to non-targeted organisms.

Project overview

Recent revelations about the dangers of pesticide use have prompted a flurry of activity looking for alternative methods of controlling pests. One area under investigation is the use of botanical (plant) products. This is not a new idea—herbs and other plant products have been used for centuries to ward off pests and disease. Today, many organic gardeners are successfully using nontoxic, botanical pesticides such as marigolds, parsnip roots, petunia leaves, and tomato plant leaves.

In this project, citrus oil, garlic, and jalapeño peppers are tested to see if they have any pesticidal qualities. The peels of lemons and other citrus fruits contain compounds called limonine and linalool. These compounds have been found to disrupt some insects' nervous systems. Garlic, when sprayed on plants, has been found to act as both an insect repellent and an antibiotic against plant disease. Capsaicin, found in jalapeño peppers, is known to be effective against ants, root maggots, and soft-bodied insects.

This project investigates the use of these three botanicals as pesticides against a common garden pest, the tomato hornworm.

Materials list

- rubber tub about the size of a shoe box—any similarly sized glass, plastic, or rubber container will work to raise the caterpillars
- tobacco hornworm eggs (available from a scientific supply house)
- tobacco hornworm growth medium (available from a scientific supply house)
- thermometer
- plastic wrap
- scissors
- 60-watt lamp
- water
- kitchen grater
- garlic
- lemon
- jalapeño peppers
- graduated cylinder
- kitchen strainer
- four large beakers (1000 ml)
- two small beakers (250 ml)

- plastic foam cooler
- stove or burner
- mineral oil
- spoon
- blender
- standard balance
- eight small plastic trays (roughly 6 cm by 12 cm and at least 3 cm high)
- labels
- stopwatch
- stirring rods

Procedures

Hatching the eggs

Follow the instructions provided with the tomato hornworm eggs. If no instructions were included, proceed as follows: Place the rubber tub under the 60-watt lamp as shown in Fig 4-1. Rest the thermometer inside the tub. Cover the tub with plastic wrap and use scissors to poke very small air holes in the wrap.

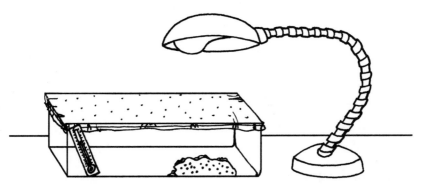

4-1 *The tub containing the insect food and eggs is placed under a lamp. Use the thermometer to assure a constant temperature.*

Adjust the height of the lamp above the tub until 27°C is reached and maintained. Place the hornworm eggs into the tub. Prepare the tomato hornworm food according to the instructions that accompanied the food. This usually involves adding a specified amount of water, mixing, and standing to cool. Place the appropriate amount of food as stated in the instructions inside the tub. Allow the larvae to feed and grow until they are 1.5 cm long before proceeding with the experiment—approximately one week. Don't throw out the remaining food; you'll use more of it later in this project.

Preparing the botanical pesticides

To prepare the citrus pesticide, finely grate the peel of one medium-size lemon. Boil 500 ml of water and add the grated peel. Boil for 10 minutes, then cover with plastic wrap and stand for 24 hours. Strain the mixture to separate the peel from the liquid; discard the peel. Label the beaker containing the remaining liquid *lemon*.

To prepare the garlic pesticide, add 30 g of minced garlic to 125 ml of mineral oil in a small beaker and stir. Cover with plastic wrap and allow the mixture to stand for 24 hours. Strain the mixture to remove pieces of garlic. Place 500 ml of water in a large beaker and add 30 ml of the garlic oil. Stir vigorously to evenly disperse the oil in the water. Take 30 ml of the oil/water mixture and dilute by adding it to another beaker containing 500 ml of water. Label this beaker *garlic*.

To prepare the jalapeño pesticide, grind 75 g of jalapeño peppers in a blender with 1000 ml of water. Strain the mixture to remove the pieces. Label this beaker *jalapeño* (see Fig. 4-2).

4-2 *Store each of the three botanical pesticides and the plain-water control in beakers.*

Creating the groups

Prepare enough hornworm medium to fill eight trays. There will be two trays for each of the four groups. Again, follow the instructions that came with the medium. Spread the hornworm medium in eight plastic trays. Label the trays as follows: *Control, Lemon, Garlic,* and *Jalapeño.*

Cover the trays with plastic wrap to lock in moisture and create a humid environment. Place the trays in an insulated container such as a plastic foam cooler (without the lid) and place a thermometer in the container. Place the apparatus under a 60-watt lamp to maintain the temperature at 27°C.

Next, add the botanical pesticides. Pour 20 ml of each pesticide mixture and spread it evenly over the properly labeled two trays. There should just be a thin layer over the medium. The control trays will receive no pesticide; instead, pour 20ml of plain water into the tray. After the pesticide is applied, place five hornworm larvae in each tray. Record the time each tray received the larvae and the immediate response of the larvae to the media.

Every 15 minutes, perform a "poke test" in which you poke the larvae with a stimulus; in this case, a stirring rod. Record the response to the poke. A healthy larvae will jerk and coil from the poke. More listless motion usually indicates a sick larva, and no response indicates a dead larva. After one hour (three poke tests from the start), continue your observations every couple of hours for 24 hours.

Analysis

How long did it take for each of the botanical pesticides to kill all of the pests? Which botanical proved the most efficient and which the least? Does it appear that natural botanicals could be used to control insect pests, at least in the house and garden?

Going further

This project involves pouring pesticide on the pest's artificial food medium. Most pesticide applications, however, spray the substance on the pest's natural food plant. Modify this project to spray the pesticide directly on a tomato plant, which is one of the hornworm's natural foods.

Alternatively, modify this project to determine the exact amounts of each pesticide needed to kill each pest.

Suggested research

- Research the use of natural botanical pesticides. Read how they have been used in the past and how they are used today.
- Research the use of garlic not only as a pesticide, but as an antibiotic.

5

Natural fertilizers

Can natural fertilizers replace synthetic fertilizers?

Background

Chemical and natural fertilizers are exact opposites. Chemical fertilizers are just that: chemicals. They are synthetic compounds designed to provide the basic nutrients to plants. Unlike natural fertilizers, they don't decompose quickly. Overapplication of these fertilizers usually results in *fertilizer runoff.* This means the fertilizer travels with runoff water after it rains and is carried to streams and rivers and finally to the ocean. Excessive amounts of these long-lived chemicals contribute to nutrient enrichment in these bodies of water. This can result in algae blooms, bacterial population explosions, and damage to the aquatic ecosystem.

In addition, synthetic fertilizers don't have the same texture as soil. After continued applications, the soil actually begins to change its structure and lose its moisture retaining abilities. The soil becomes a less attractive home to the normal community of microbes, worms, and other organisms that live there.

Project overview

Since the continuing use of synthetic fertilizers has become an environmental concern, alternatives are being studied. Natural fertilizers like compost are made of *organic* material—items that were part of a living organism not too long ago, like leaves, grass clippings, manure, household food leftovers, etc. Compost degrades rapidly so runoff is not a problem; it enhances soil texture; and maintains soil's ability to retain moisture.

The purpose of this experiment is to compare the effects of commercially available, synthetic chemical fertilizers to compost, a natural fertilizer, on the growth of bean plants. Can compost completely replace commercial fertilizer or should compost be used to supplement synthetic products?

This project requires creating compost, which takes many months. You can save this time by finding someone who already has a compost pile and asking permission to use some of their compost. The project is divided into the following parts: "Building a composter," "Sowing the seeds," "Caring for the seedlings," and "Collecting data."

Materials list

The following materials are needed to build a small compost heap. If you already have access to compost, skip the first five items.

- 6 foot × 3 foot piece of wire mesh screening with ½-inch square mesh
- small twigs
- organic materials (grass clippings, wood chips, etc.)
- garden soil
- shovel
- two packages of stringless, green pod, bush-type bean seeds
- garden sprayer or large mister
- teaspoon measure
- garden trowel
- six plastic seedling trays
- house plant fertilizer (15-30-15)
- sterilized soil (can be purchased from a scientific supply house or made on your own with an autoclave)
- ruler
- marker
- sheets of cardboard
- fourteen wooden skewer sticks
- string
- scissors
- vernier calipers

Procedures

Constructing a small compost heap

Find a convenient place to build your compost frame. It should be a good distance from homes because compost can smell and attract insects. Construct a frame out of wire mesh, 45 cm wide by 1 meter tall on each side. Turn the frame so the top and bottom are the two open ends (see Fig. 5-1). Place a layer of small twigs at the bottom, resting on the ground, for air circulation.

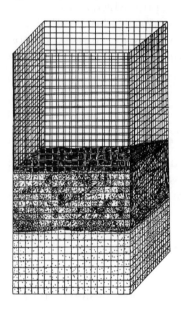

5-1
Cut the wire mesh to create your compost frame, then fill it with organic waste and soil.

Next, place a layer about 13 cm thick of organic material (i.e., grass clippings, leftover foods, garden waste, animal droppings, etc.) on the twigs. The organic matter should be in small pieces. Cover the organic waste thoroughly with about 5 cm of garden soil. Continue to add these two layers on top of the previous layers as needed.

Use the shovel to make a depression in the top of the pile to catch rain water. Water and air (from the sides and bottom) accelerate the decomposition process. Every other week, turn the compost completely over with a shovel. If you live in a very dry area, add some water to the top of the pile. Within three to six months, the pile should decompose into a rich black soil—compost.

Sowing the seeds

Label two seedling trays *Fertilizer*, two trays *Compost*, and two trays *None*. Fill all the trays to within 4 cm of the top with sterilized soil. Add to the Compost trays 2.5 cm of compost and use a garden trowel to thoroughly mix the soil and the compost.

Use your finger to make a series of holes about 2.5 cm deep for the seeds. The number of seeds you plant will depend on the size of the trays, but most can hold at least 14 seeds. Put seeds into the holes and cover with the soil.

Caring for the seedlings

Use a garden sprayer or mister to water the soil until it is moist. The Fertilizer trays should receive the appropriate amount of fertilizer according to the instructions on the container. Be sure to follow the instructions for seeds and seedlings, not for full-grown plants. The Compost and None trays receive no fertilizer. Place all the trays in the same environment and be sure they get the same amount of light and water. Follow the instructions on the seed packages for proper lighting conditions and watering.

Collecting data

Record the date when the seedlings appear through the soil. Use a ruler to measure each plant's height every other day. If necessary, straighten the stems to attain their tallest points. Measure the width and the length of the leaves. Use calipers to measure the diameter of the stems. Calculate the averages for all the plants within each group. Observe the color and general health of the plants. Record any other pertinent information such as wilting, browning, etc. Continue the observations for at least two weeks.

Analysis

Convert your data into charts for each measurement taken, as seen in Fig. 5-2. How did the three groups compare? Did the None group perform poorly compared to the other two? Did the Compost group perform as well as the commercial fertilizer? Was one group superior in all measurements to the other group or did the results vary depending on the measurement?

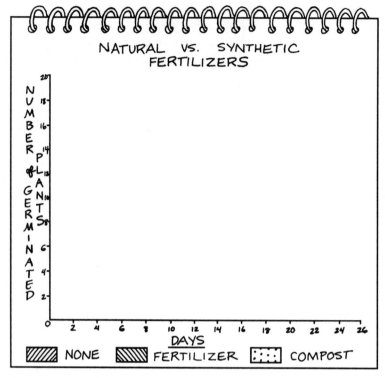

5-2 *Create a chart similar to this one to determine which type of fertilizer worked best.*

Going further

This is a laboratory test on house plants and house plant fertilizer. Devise a small field test using crop plants, fertilizers used by farmers, and compost that you created from actual wastes (e.g., grass clippings or animal manure). Include groups that not only compare all compost to all fertilizer, but also varying combinations of both.

Suggested research

- Investigate "high tech" composting. Research where the organic matter comes from and how the compost is used.
- Research the environmental and economical aspects of large scale composting.

6

Hydroponics

Does water temperature affect hydroponic plant growth?

Background

Hydroponics refers to growing plants in an artificial liquid environment. Plants that normally grow in the soil can be grown hydroponically in water containing the correct amounts and types of nutrients. Because the plants are not in soil, they require artificial support. Support is provided by some form of frame structure such as plastic tubes. The light source can be natural or artificial.

There are many reasons for choosing hydroponic plant growth, but the primary reason is space. A large number of hydroponic plants can be grown in a very small space. The growth containers can be stacked vertically upward, practically on top of one another.

Hydroponic plants are easy to care for because they don't have to be watered daily. Of course, they are always in a nutrient liquid. The liquid allows for a uniform and regulated distribution of nutrients. You don't get any leaching of minerals and nutrients as you do in soil. Hydroponics also eliminates unsightly weeds and all soilborne pests that can harm or kill plants.

Project overview

Hydroponics has become a major industry in some parts of the world. In Japan, many people have hydroponic houseplants and gardens. As with any new technology, there is always room for improvement. This experiment looks for ways to improve the growth of hydroponically grown plants. Most hydroponic plants are grown at room temperature. Would heating or cooling the liquid nutrient solution affect the growth of hydroponic plants? What is the optimal water temperature for hydroponically grown plants?

This project requires rooted cuttings from Wandering Jew house plants. It will take about two months for the cuttings to grow enough roots to do the project.

Materials list

- two 10-gallon aquarium tanks
- wire mesh screening (the mesh should be at least 2.5 cm sq so the plant cuttings can fit easily through the holes)
- wire cutters
- aquarium heater (at least one)
- aquarium thermometer (one for each tank)
- liquid houseplant food
- large potted *Tradescantia blossfeldiana*, commonly called Wandering Jew; this variety has oblong olive-green leaves with purple undersides and stems and is covered with silvery hairs (available in most garden centers)
- large potted *Tradescantia zebriana*, another variety of Wandering Jew; this variety is characterized by oval, deep green and purple leaves with two silver stripes running up the leaves (available in most garden centers)
- glass jars (at least 20)
- water
- millimeter ruler or vernier calipers
- tape
- marker

Procedures

This project has two groups and uses two tanks: a control group, which is kept at room temperature, and an experimental group, which is kept at 3°C above room temperature. If you have access to more tanks, you can have more experimental groups. For example, set up one tank 6°C cooler than room temperature; another 3°C cooler; and two tanks at temperatures warmer than room temperature.

Root the cuttings

Prepare 10 stem cuttings from each plant for each tank. (Two tanks would require 20 cuttings.) The stems should be about 30 cm long. Place the cuttings in jars of plain water to root. This will take about two months.

Prepare the tanks

Measure the dimensions of each tank. Use a wire cutter to cut the wire screening so it fits the tank as seen in Fig. 6-1. You will create a bridgelike frame that will sit in the tank to support the cuttings. Place the wire frame in one of the tanks to check the fit. There should be about a 2.5 cm clearance between the top of the frame and the top of the tank. If the first frame fits properly, create one frame for each tank.

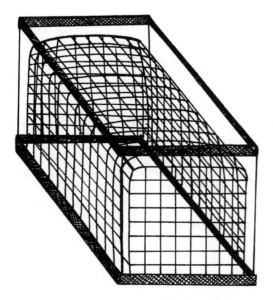

6-1
The wire mesh frame sits inside the fish tank. It will support the hydroponic plants.

Once the cuttings have established significant root growth, you can begin the experiment. Fill the tanks approximately 90% full of water and mark the water level with tape on the outside of each tank. Add the prescribed amount of plant food for 10 gallons and stir. Let the tanks sit overnight to reach room temperature. (If you are using chlorinated tap water, let them sit for 48 hours.) Place the aquarium heater in one of the tanks and set it to 6°C or 3°C higher than room temperature. Place the thermometers in each tank.

Once the water temperatures have reached the proper levels, place 10 of the *T. blossfeldiana* in every other wire space in each tank, as seen in Fig. 6-2. Fill in the remaining wire spaces with the *T. zebriana* cuttings. Alternating the cuttings assures the plants benefit from a uniform environment throughout the experiment.

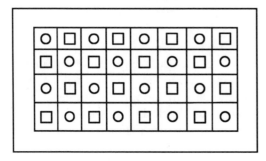

6-2
Alternate the two varieties of plants in the wire mesh squares.

☐   T. ZEBRIANA

○   T. BLOSSFELDIANA

You can use natural light or artificial lamps but all of the tanks must receive the same amount of light. Check the temperature in each tank to be sure it remains constant. Add the proper mixture of nutrient liquid to maintain the water level.

Observe

Every other day, measure the size of the smallest leaf on the top of each plant as seen in Fig. 6-3. For the *T. zebriana*, measure the space between the top three leaves and the leaf below as seen in Fig. 6-4. Look at the root structure of the plants. Observe the general health of the plants, noting any wilting, browning, etc., in each group. If you have a camera, take photographs of each tank. Continue the observations for at least two weeks.

Analysis

Does warm water benefit or harm the growth of these two hydroponically grown plants? If you used cooler water, what was its effect? Did different water temperatures appear to affect any one part of the plant, such as the leaves or roots, more than other parts?

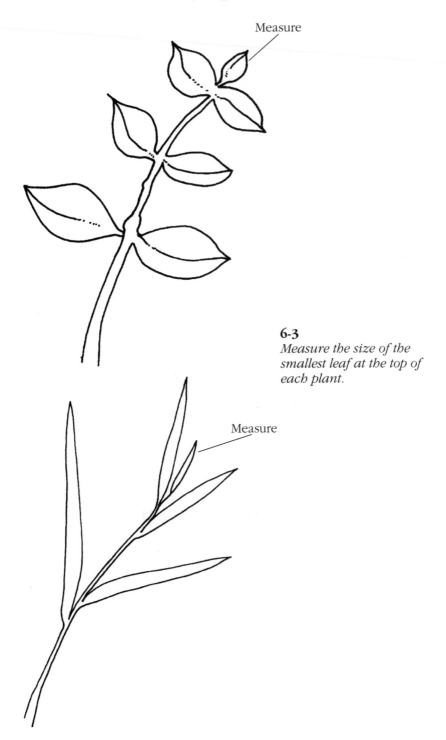

Measure

6-3
*Measure the size of the
smallest leaf at the top of
each plant.*

Measure

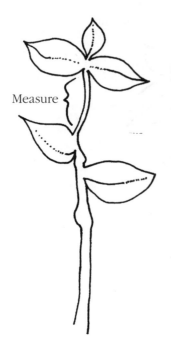

Measure {

6-4
*On the T. zebriana plants,
measure the distance
between the top three leaves
and the leaf below.*

Going further

Continue the experiment to find the optimal water temperature for each plant tested. Create a graph that illustrates the relation between water temperature and growth and points out the optimal temperature. You'll need to test a wide range of temperatures to accomplish this.

Suggested research

- Research the state of the art in hydroponic growth technology.
- Find out who is using hydroponics and why.
- Investigate the new field of hydroponic aquaculture in which fish are grown along with the plants in an artificial environment.

7

De-icing road salts

Are de-icing road salts harmful to the aquatic plant life in your town?

Background

Sodium Chloride (NaCl), or table salt, is commonly used in the winter to de-ice roads, making them safer for driving. Salt is inexpensive and does the job efficiently. Each year in New England alone, more than 10 million tons of road salt are put on more than half a million miles of roads. The salt is often applied with a mixture of sand.

The side effects of the salt applications are numerous and diverse. Salt eats away at car bodies and corrodes bridges and roads. Roads and bridges need more frequent maintenance in heavily salted areas and don't last nearly as long as structures that don't contact these salts. The most damaging effect of de-icing road salt is on the environment. The salt accumulates in gullies, streams, ponds, and lakes, seriously damaging aquatic ecosystems. It can seep into the groundwater, contaminating drinking water supplies. Salt is also harmful to roadside vegetation and the wildlife that feeds on this vegetation.

Project overview

Today there are alternatives to road salt. They are considerably more expensive, but they aren't as destructive. Calcium Magnesium Acetate (CMA) is the leading alternative to road salt and is believed to be far safer for the environment. However, some studies show that CMA might have its own set of problems. At certain temperatures, CMA might actually be harmful to the environment.

This project studies the effects of road salt and CMA on the environment. How much road salt actually gets into ponds in your area? How harmful is road salt to the environment? In particular, what effect does road salt have on the primary production (photosynthetic activity) in freshwater ponds? Is CMA less harmful to primary producers in freshwater ponds?

This project is divided into two parts. In the "Field study," you will sample roadside ponds throughout the winter after road salts are applied and measure their salinity. Once you have obtained the concentrations of salt found in these ponds, you will move on to the "Experimental study" in which you subject *chlorella*, a common freshwater alga, to the concentrations of salt actually found in the local ponds. In the "Further research" section, you can compare the results with the use of CMA instead of road salts.

Materials list

- at least four ponds located near roads that are de-iced during the winter
- twelve 50-ml polyethylene bottles
- test tube of *chlorella* stock culture (available from a scientific supply house)
- prepared culture media to grow the *chlorella* (available from a scientific supply house)
- permanent marker
- handful of road salt (available from your local Department of Public Works or Transportation)
- thirty 20–50-ml tissue culture flasks (or similar glassware to culture algae)
- deionized water
- balance or scale
- 1000 ml graduated cylinder
- autoclave
- pipettes

- 50 ml graduated cylinders
- aluminum foil
- method to measure the salinity of water (see the "Procedures" section)
- method to quantify the number of *chlorella* cells in samples (see the "Procedures" section)
- Optional: 5 g Calcium Magnesium Acetate (CMA) (possibly available from your Department of Public Works or can be ordered from a supplier; speak with your DPW to find out where it can be purchased)

Procedures

Field study

 Identify at least four ponds of varying sizes near different roads in your area. Do not use any pond situated so that it would endanger you. The ponds can be well off the shoulder of a road in a safe area. Get approval from your sponsor about the locations of all the ponds. Take a partner with you whenever you are collecting from a body of water.

To determine whether road salt (NaCl) is used for de-icing, check with your local department of public works, which is most likely responsible for maintaining the roads. Road salt is used in almost all areas.

Use the large polyethylene bottles to collect water samples from the ponds in early winter before the first snow falls. If possible, collect the samples just before the first snow falls. To obtain the samples, use a thoroughly clean 50 ml polyethylene bottle that you have rinsed with pond water. Fill the bottle with water from just below the surface. Take three samples from each pond. Label the bottles with the name of the pond. Repeat this procedure at each of the ponds.

Return to the lab with the samples to measure the salinity. There are many methods of measuring water salinity, from simple, inexpensive reagent kits to expensive meters. Any method should work, as long as it can read from 0 to 20 parts per 1000. Record the salinity for each sample.

Wait until you have had three or four snow falls and de-icing applications before taking samples again at the same locations. For best results, wait until a midwinter thaw in the weather before taking the second samples. Take samples exactly as you did the first time and use the same method to check the salinity levels of each sample.

Experimental study

Now that you know the salinity of the pond water before any winter de-icing treatments and after many de-icing applications, you can go on to the experimental portion of the project and test the effects of the salts. You will create a series of *chlorella* growth media flasks with varying concentrations of salts, as found in the first part of this project (see Fig. 7-1).

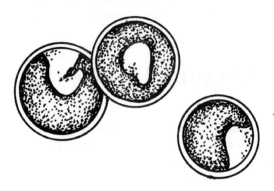

7-1
Chlorella is a common green freshwater algae found in ponds.

Adjust the algae growth medium that you've purchased or made to create six salt solutions that simulate the pond water found in the first part of the project. Each solution will be used in five flasks, so be sure to create enough of each solution.

First, select the concentrations you want to create. They should range between the lowest amount of salinity found (before de-icing) and the highest (after de-icing). For example, you might use the following concentrations: 0.5 ppt, 1 ppt, 2 ppt, 4 ppt, and 8 ppt. Also, be sure to use 0 ppt as a control.

If you are using a powdered media, the easiest way to create the various concentrations is to make the highest concentration and then dilute it down for the others. For example, add to the media the correct amount of salt to create an 8 ppt solution, then dilute it with water to 4 ppt. If you are using a prepared media, it is best to create each concentration separately. Discuss with your sponsor how to measure out the various concentrations (see Fig. 7-2).

Once you have five flasks of each concentration, dispense the *chlorella* into each flask. Thoroughly mix the original culture before dispensing a sample in each flask. Use a pipette to transfer a small amount of the original culture to each flask, making sure you add the same amount to each flask. The amount will vary depending on the size and type of flask used.

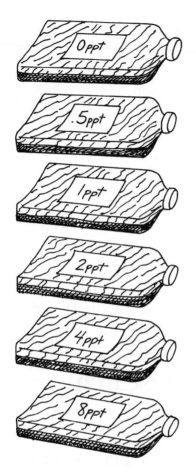

7-2
You'll create a series of de-icing salt concentrations that simulate the actual amounts found in local ponds.

Growth and observations

Once all the groups are prepared, they must be maintained in a similar environment. Ideally, this is in a growth chamber with a controlled light/dark cycle. If a growth chamber is not available, leave the culture at room temperature and follow the instructions that came with the culture and media.

Begin your observations on the first day. You can quantify the number of cells in each flask in many ways depending on the equipment available to you. Your method can be as simple as taking standard samples and counting cells, or as sophisticated as using a fluorometer, which measures the fluorescence of the contents. Speak with your advisor about the equipment available to quantify the cultures. Make observations each day. When the control group begins to die, discontinue the experiment and analyze the results.

Analysis

All food chains begin with producers. *Chlorella* is a common aquatic producer and therefore primarily responsible for the success (or failure) of many aquatic ecosystems. What effect does the application of de-icing salts on your roads have on *chlorella* living in roadside ponds? Did the concentration of salts reach a level that harmed the algae, or did the salt appear to be harmless? Would lowering the amount of salts used reduce or eliminate the problem, if one exists?

Going further

Assume your town started spreading CMA instead of road salt. Can you devise an experiment similar to this one in which you compare the effects of CMA to the results you collected here? Does CMA appear to be less harmful to the environment or does it also have problems associated with it?

You can also continue the work by studying the life cycle of the *chlorella* and its relation to the concentration of salts throughout the year in your locale.

Suggested research

- Study the impact of the collapse of a population of *chlorella* in an aquatic community. What might happen to the entire ecosystem?
- Contact those places that routinely use CMA and ask if they have seen environmental improvements.

8

Artificial coral reefs

What is the best material for artificial coral reefs?

Background

Most people have heard about the importance of tropical rain forests and wetlands. The biodiversity and abundance of life in these ecosystems is staggering. But there is another ecosystem that can match both—coral reefs. Coral reefs can be considered the tropical rain forests of the sea. Thousands of species of fish and creatures, such as sea urchin, feed on algae, bacteria, and other organisms that flourish on and around reefs.

Coral reefs are found in tropical and subtropical regions of the globe. Reefs are built primarily by coral animals, which are like tiny jellyfish. These organisms secrete calcium, which acts as a substratum (foundation) for them. It also acts as a substratum for other individuals. As the calcium deposits increase, the coral reef forms.

Project overview

Coral bleaching refers to the death of a coral reef ecosystem, which can occur due to sewage flowing into the sea from a town treatment plant; silt accumulation from soil erosion caused by agriculture, logging, or construction; or contaminants such as pesticides.

Due to the death of many coral reefs, people have become interested in creating artificial reefs. Some of these artificial reefs have successfully replaced damaged or destroyed reefs. This project investigates which material creates the best artificial reef. Does concrete, PVC pipe, wood, or aluminum work best to create a coral reef?

The student who originally performed this project actually created temporary, underwater, artificial reefs from different materials. A licensed diver was required. Because most people are not divers, you can modify the project so you don't get anything wet but your hands. For example, you could get permission to use a large marine tank at a city aquarium. Perhaps a local pet store will let you use a large (20 gal minimum) saltwater tank. In both cases, the experimental material can be lowered into the water without getting you wet. Alternately, you might be able to create a similar apparatus off a boat or along the shore. If you are a licensed diver and have access to a marine environment, discuss with your sponsor how you could perform this project.

 Under no circumstances should anyone attempt any underwater activity unless licensed to do so and under the direct supervision of your sponsor. Activity near any body of water must be done under the direct supervision of your sponsor.

The "Procedures" section provides the basic instructions for this experiment. You will have to adapt these instructions to suit your marine environment.

Materials list

- access to a marine environment as previously described
- platform to hold the materials in the water
- five equal-size pieces each of concrete block, PVC pipe, wood, and aluminum
- waterproof marker
- rope (optional)
- buoy (optional)

Procedures

Prepare the materials

All the pieces of material should be about the same size. For example, 20 sq cm blocks, pipes, and squares. If they are going into a small tank, the pieces will be much smaller—perhaps 5 cms sq for a 20 gal tank. Use a waterproof marker to draw same-size squares on the most exposed surface of each material. For example, if your block is 20 cms square, draw a 10-cm square on one side of the concrete blocks, the aluminum and wood squares, and the PVC pipes. These squares will enclose the areas used to measure the amount of plant and animal growth on each material. You should now have five pieces of each material with a square drawn on each (see Fig. 8-1).

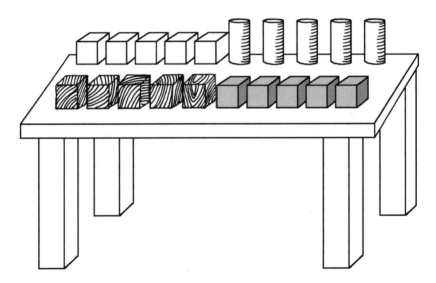

8-1 *Test five pieces of four different materials for growth.*

Next, prepare a platform to hold all of the pieces underwater. The platform must be heavy enough to remain stable. If the location of the platform is not visible (i.e., in the ocean), tie a rope and buoy to the platform so you can locate it easily. If you are doing this project in a small tank or in shallow water, this is unnecessary.

Place all the pieces of material on the platform with the drawn squares facing up. Attach the wood and aluminum squares to the platform by screwing them on or placing weights on top of them.

8-2 *The more growth found on a material, the better its chances of becoming a coral reef.*

Keep all pieces of the same material close to each other, and separate different types of materials by as much distance as possible. Put the platform into the water.

Observe the platform

Check the platform over the next few days to be sure it remains stable, then check the platform at least once a week for at least 10 weeks. After at least 10 weeks, retrieve all the materials and the platform.

Observe the amount of growth within the square areas on each piece of material. If you were using a large (more than 100 gallons) marine tank or the ocean, scrape off the material and weigh it on a scale or balance (see Fig. 8-2). The more weight, the higher the potential to become a coral reef. If you are using a small saltwater fish tank, quantify the amount of microscopic growth and use this as an indicator of coral reef potential.

Analysis

Look for the total biomass present on each type of material. Which material gathered the most living organisms? Were some materials more prone to biodiversity, meaning they had many different types of organisms?

Even if some materials showed good growth, might other factors come into play that could affect growth, such as rotting or decomposition? How would this affect the material's success as a coral reef substratum? What factors were responsible for different amounts of growth on each material?

Going further

Try to identify the organisms that were growing on each material. Use microscopic, as well as macroscopic, observations. Determine whether any material has the flora and fauna typical of a formative coral reef.

Suggested research

- Study the symbiotic relationship that exists in coral organisms.
- Study the creation of coral reefs.
- Study the destruction of coral reefs and its impact on the environment.

9

Distilled saltwater

Can distilled seawater be used to water plants?

Background

Water is our planet's most abundant natural resource and its most important. It's estimated that there are 360 billion billion gallons of water on and in our planet! But 97% of this water is saltwater, leaving only 3% fresh water—the water most life on our planet requires to survive.

Fresh water is in short supply in many regions of the world, including parts of the United States. In the southwest, states fight in court for rights to precious little water.

Project overview

The vast majority of fresh water used by man is for agriculture, specifically irrigation. Irrigation dwindles water supplies, leaving less for use in your home. Since there is no shortage of saltwater, this project investigates the potential of using distilled saltwater to grow plants.

This experiment tests whether distilled saltwater has any ill effects on plant growth. If there are no ill effects, further study can investigate the potential of using distilled water on a larger scale. If an inexpensive method could be developed to distill saltwater on a large scale, the oceans could be used to irrigate crops.

Materials list

- unit to distill saltwater (or a teapot, stove, or small glass bowl as described in the "Procedures" section)
- three glass quart jars
- ten plastic garden pots
- ruler
- potting soil
- ten similar houseplants, such as pansies
- marker
- water (well water, spring water, or tap water)
- saltwater from the ocean (if unavailable, table salt will work fine)
- graduated cylinder, beaker, or measuring cup

Procedures

Prepare the water

Fill one of the quart jars with well, spring, or tap water and label it *Control*. Fill another quart jar with ocean water. If ocean water is not available, fill this jar with the same water as the first and add ¼ cup of table salt and stir. Label this jar *Salt*.

 Next, distill the saltwater. If you are using a distillation unit, prepare 2 or 3 quarts of saltwater and distill all of it at once. If you are using a teapot, pour the saltwater into the pot, place it on the stove, and bring it to a boil. As the steam shoots out of the spout, carefully hold a small bowl over the steam. Wear an oven mitt while doing this because the steam is hot enough to burn. As the steam condenses on the bowl, angle the bowl so the moisture drips into a quart jar that you or someone else is holding below. This bowl will be to the side of the escaping stream of steam. The salt will be left in the tea pot and the quart jar will contain the distilled water. Label this quart jar *Distilled*.

You will use the Distilled jar and the Control jar to water two groups of five plants. Keep the jar you labeled Salt because you will have to repeat the distillation process when the water runs out.

Prepare the plants

All of the potted plants should be of similar height and general health before beginning. Mark five potted plants *Control/1* through *Control/5* and the other five, *Distilled/1* through *Distilled/5*. Record the height of each plant and note the general condition of all. All of the plants should be kept under identical light conditions and all must receive the same amount of water.

Water each plant with the exact amount each day; use a graduated cylinder, beaker, or measuring cup. The control group receives water from the Control jar and the distilled group receives water from the Distilled jar. The amount of water dispensed should be determined by the size of the plants and the pots.

Observe

Make observations every two days over a period of three or more weeks depending on the type of plant used. If the plants have grown buds and are about to flower, continue the project until after they flower. At the conclusion of the growth period, record the height of the plants, the number of leaves, and the general color of the leaves. You can also measure the diameter of the stems and remove the plants from the soil to measure their wet weights. Include observations about any flowers that might have bloomed.

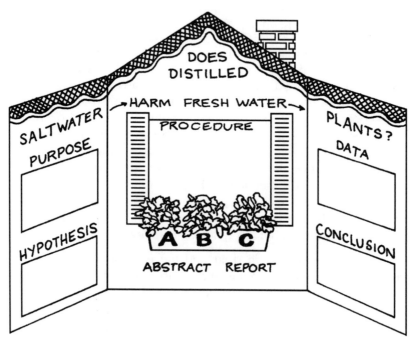

9-1 *Here is an interesting idea for your project's backboard.*

Analysis

Convert your raw data into graphs as shown in Fig. 9-2. Compare the control with the distilled group. Did the experimental group fair as well? Does it appear that distilled saltwater could be used to grow plants?

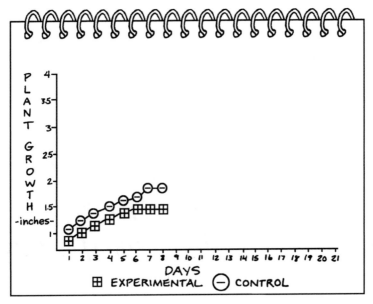

9-2 *Create a chart similar to this one to illustrate your data.*

Going further

You can continue the project by performing small field tests on crops. If you have a garden, divide it into tracts and continue the project in the field. Alternately, does the saltwater have to be completely distilled? Continue the project, but see if partially distilled water, which might be more economical to produce, can be used to successfully grow plants.

Suggested research

- If your results indicated that distilled water can be used to grow plants, is this process being used anywhere on a large scale? If so, where, and if not, why not?
- Investigate marine plant life. How do marine plants thrive in saltwater environments? Study the structure and physiology of these plants.

10

Compost as a fertilizer

Can compost replace or supplement commercial fertilizers?

Background

Recycle and *compost* are two terms you often hear today when discussing solutions to environmental problems. Most people don't realize that composting is the earth's method of recycling.

After we use manufactured glass, aluminum, or plastic products, we recycle them into raw material to create new bottles, cans, etc. When an animal such as a cow eats grass, some of the food is used by the animal, but most exits as waste. A cow flop in a field is broken down by fungi, bacteria, insects, and the weather until it decomposes back to basic compounds. These organic substances act as a natural fertilizer to grow more grass. The same thing happens to animals and plants that die in the field or forest. They decompose to provide fertilizer for plants.

Compost doesn't have to come from cow flops or dead plants and animals. It could come from leftover foods. Scraps of fruits, vegetables, bread, and just about any other food will decompose into a rich fertilizer.

Through the process of composting, we try to accelerate the natural process of decomposition. Instead of waiting for the decomposition process to proceed at its own pace, we create the best environment for it to occur. Composting involves providing as much air and water as possible to accelerate the decomposition process.

Project overview

What happens to our garbage? Most of it goes into landfills, but landfills are closing at a dramatic rate because they are full or are polluting our drinking water when they leak. What to do with our waste has become a major environmental dilemma.

A large percentage of municipal solid waste is organic, meaning it can be composted into fertilizer, which can in turn be used to grow crops. Using compost as a fertilizer reduces our dependence on both landfills and expensive synthetic fertilizers. The fertilizers most farmers spread on their crops and you spread on your lawn are not natural products. They destroy the texture of the soil and leave it prone to erosion.

Because compost is natural, it enriches the soil with nutrients and maintains its natural texture and water retention capabilities. Using more compost and less synthetic fertilizer is a solution that will probably become more popular in the near future.

In this project, you'll test the effectiveness of compost used in conjunction with synthetic commercial fertilizers on growing plants. Can compost replace commercial fertilizers entirely, or is it most effective when used in conjunction with commercial fertilizers?

Materials list

- compost (homemade compost or purchased from a garden center)
- seeds (any type—bean or tomato seeds work well)
- thirty-six seedling pots
- potting soil for all the pots
- two watering cans with measurement units (or beaker to measure the liquid)
- commercial synthetic fertilizer (one that can be mixed with water)
- ruler

- vernier calipers
- garden spade
- marker

Procedures

Prepare the pots
Label six pots as follows: 0%, 10%, 25%, 50%, 75%, and 100%, as seen in Fig. 10-1. These percentages refer to the amount of compost in each pot. For example, the 25% pot contains 25% compost and 75% soil. Create two more sets of six pots with the same labels for a total of 18 pots.

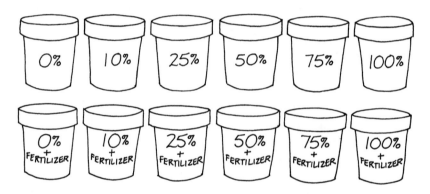

10-1 *Create three sets of six pots containing a compost/soil mixture and another three sets of six pots containing a compost/soil plus fertilizer mixture.*

Next, create three more sets with similar labels but add *+Fertilizer* to each as seen in the figure. You now have six sets of six pots; half contain compost plus fertilizer and half contain only compost.

Add to each pot the amount of compost indicated on the label. For example, fill the 25% pot one-quarter full with compost. Do this for all of the pots in all of the groups. The 0% pots are left empty. Then fill the remainder of each pot with potting soil and use the garden spade to thoroughly turn and mix the compost and the potting soil.

Use your finger to poke a hole 2 cm deep in the center of each pot; bury one seed in each hole. Tap down the soil and create a small well to retain water. After you have planted all of the seeds, prepare for watering and fertilizing.

Water the plants

Label one of the watering cans *Water* and the other *Water+Fertilizer*. The compost-only pots will be watered with the Water can and the +Fertilizer pots will be watered with the Water+Fertilizer can. All pots should receive the same amount of water each day. Prepare the Water+Fertilizer can according to the directions on the fertilizer label.

Water all of the pots using the correct watering can. All the pots should be placed in the same environment. They should all get the same amount of sun and be in the same room to assure the humidity level is consistent. Record the date when the seedlings break the surface of the soil. Then take the following readings every other day: a) use a ruler to measure height; b) use the vernier calipers to measure the diameter of the stems; and c) record the number and color of leaves and the number of flowers produced, if any.

Analysis

Use the data to create graphs similar to those in Fig. 10-2. Look at all the possible combinations. Study the groups as a continuum by starting with the pots containing no compost and no fertilizer. Then look at the pots with no compost plus fertilizer, then 10% compost and no fertilizer. Continue as the percentages increase.

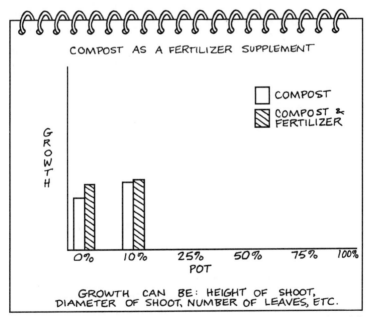

10-2 *Create a chart similar to this one to illustrate the differences in plant growth between groups.*

Compare the results of each combination. Is 10% compost plus no fertilizer as good as 0% compost plus fertilizer? Create a ratio between the amount of compost needed to eliminate a certain amount of fertilizer, yet still produce the same plant growth.

Does it appear that compost can replace commercial fertilizers without reducing plant yields? Create a chart to illustrate this relationship.

Going further

This experiment was done in the lab on potted plants. Take it a step further and reproduce it on small garden plots under more realistic conditions. Consider creating a series of plots similar to the one in Fig. 10-3. Notice each plot has a buffer zone to protect it from the other plots.

PLOT DESIGN

buffer	0/100	buffer	80/0	buffer	80/100	buffer
buffer	20/100	buffer	40/100	buffer	20/0	buffer
buffer	40/0	buffer	60/0	buffer	100/0	buffer
buffer	0/0	buffer	100/100	buffer	60/100	buffer
buffer	60/0	buffer	0/0	buffer	20/0	buffer
buffer	80/0	buffer	60/100	buffer	40/0	buffer
buffer	20/100	buffer	0/100	buffer	80/100	buffer
buffer	40/100	buffer	100/100	buffer	100/0	buffer
buffer	60/100	buffer	100/0	buffer	80/100	buffer
buffer	40/0	buffer	20/100	buffer	0/0	buffer
buffer	100/100	buffer	0/100	buffer	80/0	buffer
buffer	20/0	buffer	40/0	buffer	60/0	buffer

** compost / commercial fertilizer **

10-3 *You can create an experimental plot in your garden. Be sure to include buffer zones between the different groups.*

Alternately, you could modify the source of the compost. Use one compost created from household food wastes and another from cattle feed wastes. Does one produce better compost than the other?

Suggested research

- Research the current use of compost on the farm and in the garden. It's one thing for it to work, but it's another for it to be economically feasible.
- Look into the company that makes ZooDoo. How are they helping to solve a unique segment of our waste disposal problem and making a profit in doing so? Contact ZooDoo at 1-800-I-LUV-DOO.

Part 3

The Assault on Plants

This section helps you investigate how environmental problems are damaging plants. The projects try to quantify the damage. There are two unique projects about acid rain. Chapter 11 studies the effects of direct contact between acid rain and plants, and Chapter 13 investigates where acid rain is coming from in your location.

There are two projects on ultra-violet radiation. Chapter 14 studies its effects on aquatic, unicellular plants, and Chapter 16 investigates its effects on terrestrial plants.

Chapter 15 looks at the effects of detergents on plant growth, and Chapter 12 quantifies the effects of electromagnetic radiation on algae growth.

11

Acid rain and direct contact

Does direct contact of acid rain on bean plants harm growth?

Background

Acid rain has become an environmental problem on a global scale. The two main components of acid rain are nitric acid and sulfuric acid. Both are formed by burning fossil fuels, which release pollutants into the atmosphere. Electric power plants and automobile exhausts are the major contributors to this problem.

Under natural circumstances, water merges with carbon dioxide in the atmosphere to create a weak acid. Therefore, normal rainwater is slightly acidic, with a pH value of about 5.6. When pollutants from burning fossil fuels are emitted into the atmosphere, a series of reactions occur resulting in the formation of additional acids, resulting in acid rain.

The pH scale is logarithmic. A value of 7 on the pH scale is neutral. Each unit (whole number) on this scale is 10 times greater or less than the next whole number. Therefore a pH of 5 is 10 times more acidic than a pH of 6. The scale ranges from 1, the most acidic, to 14, the most basic.

Project overview

We know that acid rain damages aquatic ecosystems. The impact of acid rain on terrestrial vegetation and forestry is still controversial, but most scientists believe there is a direct link between declining terrestrial ecosystems and acid rain.

Most of the studies about the effects of acid rain investigate the absorption of the acid rain through plant roots. The purpose of this project, however, is to see if the leaves of plants are damaged when they come in direct contact with acid rain and whether increased acidic conditions cause more damage.

Symptoms of damaged leaf structure include necrosis (decaying) of the leaves, lesions on the leaves, and *chlorosis*, which is a discoloration of the leaves due to a loss in chlorophyll. Does acid rain cause any or all of these symptoms?

Materials list

- forty-five plastic plant pots (0.5 l or smaller)
- bean seeds
- potting soil for all the pots: spagnum moss, processed bark, and vermiculite
- three plastic troughs (each will hold about 15 pots and catch water)
- bleach
- pH meter or pH paper
- craft sticks or wood stakes to support plants
- string
- four acid-proof spray bottles
- funnel
- three glass bottles with screw caps
- microscope
- dissecting scope
- microscope slides
- cover slips
- refrigerator
- sharp hobby knife
- pipettes
- textbook showing the structure of a typical healthy bean (or similar) plant leaf

To prepare acid rain solutions, you will need the following ingredients. You can purchase premixed sulfuric acid solutions to eliminate the need for concentrated sulfuric acid and sodium hydroxide.

Preparing and using simulated acid rain solutions involves very dangerous chemicals. All work must be done with your sponsor. Wear goggles, gloves, and protective clothing at all times.

- three 1000-ml beakers
- spin plate
- stir bar
- distilled water
- concentrated sulfuric acid
- sodium hydroxide

Procedures

Planting seeds

Create a solution of 10% bleach to 90% water. Soak the seeds in this solution overnight to kill any surface bacteria. Fill at least 45 pots with potting soil. Fill 15 with sphagnum peat moss, 15 with processed bark, and the remaining 15 with vermiculite. Fill all the pots to the same height within each pot. Plant the seeds 2.5 cms deep in the potting soil. Water all the seeds with the same amount of water each day.

Allow the plants to reach at least 8 cm in height before continuing with the project. Select at least 12 plants from each group that are all about the same size and health. Each group of 12 should be divided into four pH sections. Label three pots within each group *2.5*, three pots *3.0*, three pots *3.5*, and the final three *Control.*

Making acid rain solutions

 If you have purchased premixed solutions of sulfuric acid, skip this section. This section must be performed under the supervision of your sponsor. You must wear goggles, gloves, and protective clothing when handling sulfuric acid and the diluted solutions.

Put a 100 ml beaker on a spin plate. Fill the beaker with distilled water. Place the stir bar in the beaker. Turn on the spin plate so the spin bar rotates in a circular motion, mixing the solution. This assures the acid is uniformly distributed throughout the solution when you take pH readings.

If you are using a pH meter, calibrate it to tap water. Place one drop of sulfuric acid in the beaker, wait for the mixing action to distribute the acid, then take a reading. If you are using a meter, wait for the meter to stabilize. You want to create three solutions, one each at pH levels of 2.5, 3.0, and 3.5.

If the pH level must be lowered, add another drop of sulfuric acid. If the pH level is too low, add drops of sodium hydroxide until the pH level reaches the required level. Repeat this process until you have three beakers, each containing the required pH level.

Store the three acids in clean glass bottles with screw caps. Clearly label the bottles and place them under refrigeration. These bottles will supply the simulated acid rain for the project. The liquids will be transferred into spray bottles when you are ready to begin.

Applying acid rain to the plants

Transfer each acid solution into a spray (mister) bottle. Be sure the spray bottle and nozzle can withstand the acids. Label the spray bottles clearly and keep them in the refrigerator when not in use. Spray (mist) all the leaves on each plant with the correct pH level for its group. Twice per day for at least five days, spray each plant until the leaves are saturated.

 When spraying the acid solutions, wear goggles, gloves, and protective clothing. Spray the control group of plants with distilled (neutral) water.

The plants will be weighed down by the mist, and you might need to prop them up with supporting poles. Water the roots with tap water each day as needed but use the same amount of water on all the plants each day.

Making observations

First, look at the overall health of the plants. Make observations about the condition of the plants within each group. Measure height, number of leaves, brown spots, etc. (see Fig. 11-1). Refer to an illustration of a typical healthy leaf. Next, look at the gross structure of the leaves with a dissecting microscope. Begin with the control group. Look for differences between the control group and each of the experimental groups. Look at structures on both sides of the leaves.

Finally, look at the microscopic structures by removing one square cm piece of tissue from the leaves of each plant. Use a sharp hobby knife to cut out the tissue. Place the tissue on a glass slide and add one drop of water. Cover the tissue with a coverslip and examine under a light microscope. Look for microscopic lesions. Record the size and number of these lesions, if any. Look for the stomata (see Fig. 11-2). Try to prepare a slide containing a section thin enough to view in cross-section.

11-1 *Look for lesions caused by the acid rain on the surface of the leaves.*

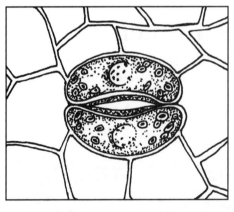

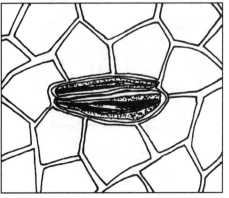

11-2 *Full-sized guard cells indicate a healthy leaf, whereas shriveled guard cells might indicate acid rain damage.*

Cut at least three samples from each pot and record the lesions for each plant to get group averages. Look at the structure around the lesions. For example, look for signs of chlorosis, a lack of green color due to a loss of chlorophyll.

Analysis

How did the different pH levels affect the growth of the plants overall? Were there any gross structural differences between plants sprayed with acids of different pH levels when you looked under the dissecting scope? Most important, how did the microscopic structure of the leaves differ? Did the acid corrode the tissues? Did it cause chlorosis or necrosis? Did the acid attack the cuticle layer (waxy coating), penetrate the epidermal layer (uppermost layer of cells), and/or harm the inner tissues? Examine the stomata and their guard cells. Were they damaged or shriveled in any of the plants? Did more acidic conditions cause more harm or did there appear to be a point when the damage plateaued?

Going further

If you can get access to a scanning electron microscope (SEM), observe the leaf tissue damage under it and look for more exacting damage (see Fig. 11-3). Some companies, universities, or science museums allow students to utilize their SEM equipment under their close supervision for research.

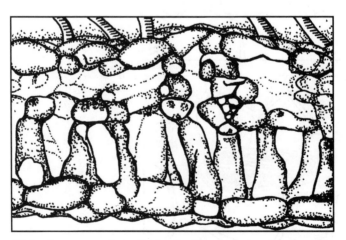

11-3 *A cross section of a leaf will reveal the details of the damage.*

Alternately, continue this project, but use finer differences between the pH levels. Look for the optimal pH level for certain houseplants. Might misting of some houseplants with a slightly acidic or basic solution improve their growth?

Suggested research

- Read the latest studies about acid rain and the controversy that surrounds this subject. Look into studies that concentrate on direct contact.
- Most of the research on acid rain centers on environmental problems. Read about the human health problems that some scientists believe are caused by acid rain.

12

Electromagnetic radiation and algae

Is electromagnetic radiation harmful to algae?

Background

Anything connected to an electric circuit produces both an electric field and a magnetic field. This includes the immediate area around household items such as electric blankets, personal computers, and electric alarm clocks. It also includes a much larger area around the high-tension power lines that crisscross the country.

Some research indicates that this radiation might pose a health risk. But it seems for every study indicating a health hazard, there are contradictory studies that state there is no health risk.

Project overview

Most of the research on power lines has concentrated on the magnetic portion of this radiation, not the electric radiation. Many of the studies about electromagnetic radiation (EMR) have investigated its effects on people who have been exposed to EMR over long periods of time. For example, people working in close proximity to sources of EMR. Other studies have investigated whether there are health risks to other organisms, both terrestrial and aquatic. If other forms of life are harmed by this radiation, should we be concerned about our own health?

How does EMR affect algae? Algae is responsible for the primary production in many bodies of water. If it is affected by EMR, how might it affect an entire aquatic ecosystem? If algae is harmed by EMR, might humans also suffer?

In this project, you will build an apparatus to hold algae in electromagnetic fields of varying strengths to see if the algae is affected.

Materials list

- algae (best if purchased from a scientific supply house to ensure you are dealing with one type of algae; you can, however, collect your own from a local pond)
- 75 ft of #18 gauge, single-conductor, insulated, solid copper wire
- 13.3 ft of 1-x-3-in wood strapping
- screwdriver
- wood screws
- flat piece of Plexiglas (2.5 × 38 in)
- duplex outlet box and receptacle (available from an electrical supply store)
- plastic wire cap nuts
- clock/timer
- sander/file
- gaussmeter (measures EMR; can be rented or borrowed; try your local utility company)
- electric or hand drill with bits to drill through the wood and the Plexiglas
- two bulb fixtures
- grow bulbs
- eyedropper
- microscope
- microscope slides
- test tubes
- spring water

Procedures

Construct the frame

First construct a wood frame to hold the test tubes, as seen in Figs. 12-1 and 12-2. The electrical wiring for this structure is illustrated in Fig. 12-3. Cut the 1-x-3-inch wood strapping into the following lengths: two 39-inch pieces for the top and bottom of the frame; two 24-inch pieces for the sides; two 12-inch pieces for the stands; two 1-inch pieces for the Plexiglas side supports; and one 8-inch piece for the Plexiglas middle support.

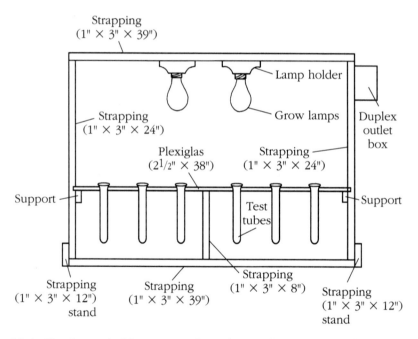

12-1 *The frame holds six test tubes, electrical wiring, and fixtures to test the effects of varying levels of electromagnetic radiation on algae.*

Use wood screws to frame all the pieces in place according to the two figures. Then prepare the Plexiglas by drilling six holes evenly spaced across the sheet. The sheet will act as a test tube holder so make sure the holes accommodate the test tubes as seen in the figure. Affix the Plexiglas in the frame. The Plexiglas is suspended by the two side support blocks and the middle strapping. The entire apparatus is supported by the two perpendicular support strips (see Fig. 12-2). When the structure is complete, place a test tube in each hole.

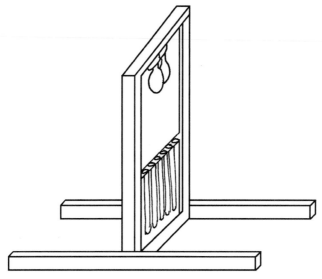

12-2 *The entire frame is supported by these per-pendicular strips.*

Prepare the wiring

Next, prepare the electrical apparatus as seen in Fig. 12-3. First, attach a duplex outlet box to the side of the frame as seen in the figure. Fasten the two bulb fixtures to the top of the frame. If the fixtures are not already wired, do so now by using the proper gauge lamp cord wire and plugs, which will be plugged into the outlet box attached to the frame.

Now you'll need to create the wire that will produce the EMF around the test tubes. Leave one meter of slack at one end of the #18 gauge, single conductor, insulated, solid copper wire. At the 1 meter mark, wrap the wire around the first test tube (#1) 75 times as seen in the figure. Leave enough slack for the wire to go to the adjacent test tube (#2), then wrap the wire around this tube 60 times. Repeat this procedure for each test tube with number #3 wrapped 45 times; #4 wrapped 30 times; #5 wrapped 15 times; and #6 wrapped 5 times.

Wrap and attach the remaining portion of the wire along the side and top of the frame so it reaches the duplex outlet box. Cut the wire and strip 2.5 cms of insulation from the end. Attach the wire to the proper screw. Strip insulation from the other end of the cut wire and attach to the other screw. Attach the remainder of this wire to the frame as seen in Fig 12-3. You are now left with the two ends of the wire—the one that just passed in and out of the duplex outlet box and the end you started with. These two ends are used to create a wall plug. A simple way to do this is to connect the two ends of wire

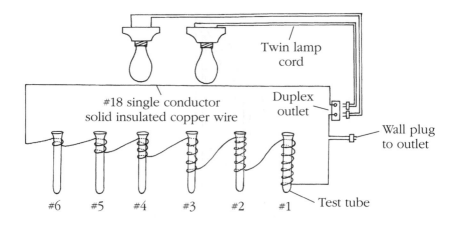

Wiring diagram

12-3 *This is the electrical schematic for the frame.*

with two ends of a split lamp cord using plastic wire cap nuts. Attach the split lamp cord to a plug if it is not already attached.

Next, screw the grow bulbs into the fixtures attached earlier to the top of the frame. You'll also need light on the side of the test tubes, so place a grow lamp fixture on the side of the apparatus so it shines evenly on the six test tubes.

 Have this entire circuit thoroughly checked by your teacher, sponsor, or other individual knowledgeable about electrical circuits before plugging it into a wall outlet.

The apparatus is set. Plug the bulb fixtures (on the top of the frame) into the outlet box on the side of the frame and insert the plug that you created earlier into a wall socket. This should turn on the grow lamps on the top and create an electromagnetic field around the test tubes. You must also turn on the grow lamps on the side of the apparatus.

Use the gaussmeter to take readings immediately adjacent to each test tube. Following the instructions that came with the meter, hold the meter next to each tube and record the level. EMF is highly directional, so follow the instructions about turning the meter in different directions when taking readings. Those test tubes surrounded by the most coils should produce the highest readings and those with the fewest coils should produce the lowest. Once this is confirmed, you can begin the actual experiment.

Add the algae and observe

Thoroughly mix your algae population in its container. Immediately after mixing, use an eyedropper or pipette to transfer 10 ml of algae and its medium to each test tube. Fill each test tube with spring water to the same height. Use a ruler to measure the distance from the top of each tube. Record the time the experiment begins.

Remove some additional algae and observe it under the microscope. Refer to a reference book that illustrates the structure of normal algal cells. Draw illustrations of what you see.

After running the apparatus for 12 hours, take samples from each test tube with the dropper or pipette and note any changes that have occurred. Look carefully at the cell walls and the location of the chlorophyll. Take detailed notes about the samples from each test tube. Continue the project by taking samples and making observations every six hours. Continue until you no longer see changes occurring.

Analysis

Did you notice any structural differences in algal cells from each test tube? Did cells in any test tube have deformities, ruptured cell walls, or displaced chlorophyll? If so, did you find many such cells? If damaged cells were found, did the severity of the damage or the number of the damaged cells increase with increased levels of radiation? Does it appear that electromagnetic radiation damages algal cells? Do you think that more radiation causes more harm?

Going further

This experiment deals with structural damage to individual algal cells. Modify the experiment to study the effect of electromagnetic radiation on the entire population of algae. How does EMR affect population growth? This project did not have a true control test tube. Modify the project to include a control that is subjected to absolutely no EMR.

Modify the project to include a far wider range of radiation fields. Does electromagnetic radiation affect algae in nature? Devise a project to answer this question.

Suggested research

- Research the latest studies about the health effects of EMR on people.

- Research the effects of EMR on other organisms and ecosystems in their entirety.
- Study how EMR is controlled within the home by contacting the Institute of Baubiologie in Clearwater, Florida.

13

The origins of acid rain

Is there a connection between acid rain and wind currents in your hometown?

Background

When fossil fuels are burned, they release pollutants into the air. Some of these pollutants react with one another in the presence of the sun to produce acids. When these acids fall to the earth with rain, it is called acid rain. Normal rain is slightly acidic, with a pH of about 5.6. Each unit on the pH scale is 10 times greater or less than the next unit. In other words, 4.6 is 10 times more acidic than 5.6. Rainfall in New England and adjoining parts of Canada is often in the 4.0 to 4.5 pH range, which is the acidity of grapefruit juice. Rainfall collected on mountain tops in New Hampshire has been recorded at a pH level of 2.1, which is the acidity of lemon juice.

Acid rains are known to damage aquatic and terrestrial ecosystems and might be responsible for some lung ailments in people. Although the exact amount of damage caused by acid rain is unknown, we know it is harming our global environment and will get worse unless pollutants are controlled.

Project overview

The pollutants produced by burning fossil fuels float through the atmosphere and are carried by the westerly winds. Some rural areas with no industry and few cars have the worst acid rain because they are routinely downwind from the source responsible for the pollutants.

This project helps you determine the source of acid rain in your town. You will compare the wind currents in your town with the acidity of the rainwater that falls over a period of time. Where is the air coming from that blows acid rain your way? Does your area only get acid rain during certain weather patterns? Does the temperature or local wind direction make a difference?

Materials list

- pH tester (an inexpensive kit from a pet store should work fine)
- weather page from your local newspaper for a period of many months (The paper should show the wind current at the regional or national level and give the daily temperatures and local wind direction.)
- ceramic container with a flat bottom
- distilled water
- paper towels
- centimeter ruler

Procedures

During this project, you will collect precipitation samples and record information from the weather page of your local paper (or television weather) every day for at least one month, but preferably many months (see Fig. 13-1). The longer the duration of the project, the more accurate the results.

Measuring rain

Place the ceramic bowl outside, exposed to the elements. After each precipitation event, measure the amount of water in the ceramic bowl to half a centimeter. Document 2 cm and less as a Low Event; 2.5 to 3 cm as a Medium Event; and greater than 3 cm as a High Event.

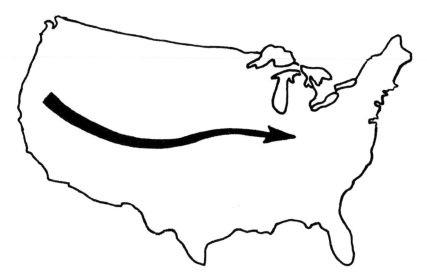

13-1 *Follow your newspaper's weather map for many months to track the direction of the wind currents.*

Record the type of event and its date in your log book, as seen in Fig. 13-2. Bring the bowl inside and wait until it reaches room temperature. Then use the pH tester to measure the pH of the water; record the pH.

Check the paper for the wind current map. Are the currents coming up from the south, down from the north, or directly from the west? Record this information. Record the local wind direction (this is not necessarily the same as the currents), the air temperature, the type of precipitation, and any additional comments. After each event, rinse the bowl out with distilled water, dry with a paper towel, and return it outside to the same location.

Information is recorded only after precipitation events. Depending on your location, you might be collecting data every couple of days or once every few weeks. Remember, the more collection days the better. In some portions of the country, the project should continue for many months.

Analysis

After collecting the data, study the wind current direction and the pH of all the events. Does there appear to be a connection between the two? Is your town drenched in acid rains when the currents are blowing from a certain direction? What is the source of the pollutants com-

ACID RAIN RAW DATA

EVENT DATE	PRCP TYPE	PH	PREC SOURCE	WIND DIR	AIR TEMP	COMMENTS
04/07/94	DR	4.8	N	NE	50	
04/08/94	SW	4.8	N	N	46	
04/18/94	SW	5.5	S	SW	57	
04/23/94	DR	5.7	S	SE	58	
04/26/94	SW	4.8	N	NW	55	
04/27/94	SW	5.0	W	W	60	
04/28/94	SW	5.7	W	W	51	
05/05/94	DR	4.9	N	SE	58	
05/06/94	DR	4.8	N	N	59	
05/09/94	TH	4.8	N	S	70	
05/10/94	TH	6.0	S	SW	69	
05/17/94	TH	4.8	N	N	68	
05/18/94	TH	5.2	E	SE	64	
05/19/94	TH	4.8	E	E	65	DRIZZLE FOLLOWED THUNDERSTORM
05/24/94	TH	4.9	N	SW	67	
06/02/94	DR	4.8	N	NE	66	
06/03/94	DR	5.7	S	E	58	
06/09/94	TH	4.8	N	NE	62	DRIZZLE FOLLOWED THUNDERSTORM

13-2 *Fill in a log book with the date of the precipitation event, type of precipitation, pH of the precipitation, wind currents, local wind direction, air temperature, and any other comments.*

ing from that direction? Is your rain less acidic when the winds are blowing from another direction?

Also study the relationship between air temperature and acid rain. Is there a connection? Study the relationship between the local winds and acid rain. Is there a connection?

Going further

Continue your analysis by looking for relationships you might not have considered. For example, is there a link between long, dry spells and the acidity of the first rains to fall after the drought? Is there a relationship between the type of precipitation and the acidity? For example, does hail appear to be as acidic as rain?

You can also continue this project by mapping out the region where most of your acid rain comes from and then investigating the causes of the pollutants. What industry or commercial centers are found in that region?

Suggested research

- Research the sources of acid rain at a national level and see how your location fits into the big picture.
- Contact the National Oceanic and Atmospheric Administration in Washington, D.C. for information about tracking acid rains.
- Investigate what is being done about acid rain by contacting The Acid Rain Foundation, Inc. in St. Paul, Minnesota.

14

Holes in the ozone and unicellular organisms

Does short-term exposure to ultraviolet light affect Euglena?

Background

Ultraviolet (UV) light is found beyond the violet end of the visible light spectrum (see Fig. 14-1). This invisible light comes primarily from the sun but it is also produced by lightning in the atmosphere. Ultraviolet light causes sunburn and has been linked to skin cancer and genetic damage. Ultraviolet light doesn't just cause problems to humans, however. Ultraviolet radiation with wavelengths less than 300 nanometers kills bacteria and viruses.

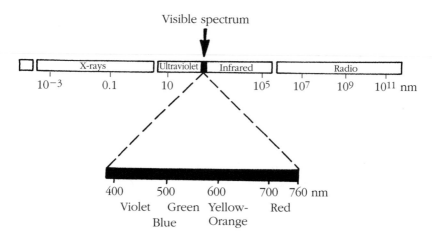

14-1 *Ultraviolet radiation is just beyond violet in the visible light spectrum.*

Hospitals use UV light in germicidal lamps to sterilize surgical equipment. Some food and drug companies use UV radiation to disinfect products, containers, and equipment.

Project overview

The ozone layer absorbs most of the UV rays that approach the earth, helping to keep radiation at safe levels for life on our planet. The use of refrigerants and aerosol products, however, has caused holes in the ozone layer. These holes have increased the amounts of UV radiation reaching some portions of the earth. Because excessive amounts of UV radiation can cause health problems, the damage to the ozone layer has heightened our awareness about UV radiation.

The effect of increased levels of UV radiation on our global ecosystem is a hot topic of study. Which organisms are the most prone to harm and which are safe from harm? This project uses a fascinating protist that is part animal and part plant—the unicellular *Euglena*. This one-celled organism moves about like an animal, but contains chloroplasts and performs photosynthesis like plants. Is UV radiation harmful to this organism? If UV does harm Euglena, should we worry about its effect on humans?

Materials list

- Euglena gracilis culture (available from a scientific supply house)

- incubator (optional)
- source(s) of UV light (you need a lamp or lamps capable of producing both short (250 nanometer) and long (365 nanometer) waves—speak with your sponsor about where you can borrow these lamps)
- test tubes
- test tube racks
- microscope
- beakers
- graduated cylinders
- microscope slides
- coverslips
- graduated pipette

Procedures

You must maintain a pure culture of Euglena throughout this experiment. Follow the instructions that came with the culture. Although you can maintain a colony without an incubator, Euglena will thrive if maintained in an incubator between 20°C and 23°C. Once you have a thriving colony, begin the project.

Use a pipette to transfer 5 mls of the Euglena culture into each of two test tubes. Label these tubes *Exp1*. Place the tubes in a test tube rack. Wait about 15 minutes to give the organisms time to acclimate themselves, then take a small sample from each of the tubes and observe under the microscope. Notice the movement of the organisms and record this activity. Also note the sediment at the bottom of the tubes. This is time 0, which acts as the control.

Next, hold the short-wave UV lamp 10 cms away from the test tubes for two minutes. Remove the lamp and take a few small samples from both tubes. Record the movement you see and the color of the water. Place 10 mls of culture in each of two new test tubes and label them *Exp2*. Repeat the exposure procedure but keep the tubes under the UV lamp for four minutes before making your observations. Continue this process to at least a 20 minute application of short-wave UV radiation. Then repeat the entire process, but use the long-wave UV lamp.

Create a chart similar to Fig. 14-2 that shows changes in the organisms' movement and the sediment in the bottoms of the tubes after varying amounts of UV exposure.

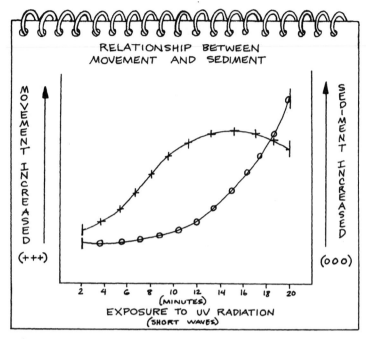

14-2 *Illustrate your data with a chart similar to this one.*

Analysis

Did the presence of UV radiation change the movement patterns of the Euglena? Did the different wave lengths make a difference? Did longer durations of exposure cause changes in movement? If there was a relationship between the UV exposure and movement, does it mean the radiation is beneficial or harmful to the organisms?

Did the amount of sediment at the bottom of the tubes change with exposure to radiation? What was the sediment composed of? What can you conclude about the immediate effects of UV radiation on these plantlike organisms?

Going further

This project looks at short-term intense exposure to UV radiation. Modify the project to study longer-term exposure to more realistic, natural levels of UV radiation. Can small changes in the amount of UV radiation (as is occurring today due to ozone depletion) have a negative impact on Euglena?

Continue this project but collect your own microbial pond life. How does UV radiation effect algae, diatoms, and other protists?

Suggested research

- Study ozone depletion, increased UV radiation levels, and the harm it is causing or could cause in the future to people and other animals as well as to plants.
- Study the structure of the Euglena. Why has this organism been a problem for taxonomists?

15

Detergents and plant growth

What is the effect of detergents on plant growth?

Background

In the natural world, a dynamic balance exists between the amount of nutrients and minerals entering an ecosystem and the amount used by that ecosystem. These substances are used by producers during photosynthesis and are passed along food chains to consumers to be recycled as waste or decomposing organisms, resupplying the natural nutrients for another generation of organisms.

When human intervention changes the quantity of nutrients and minerals entering an ecosystem, equilibrium is lost and the natural order is destroyed. We change the composition of nutrients and minerals in ecosystems in many ways. The two major processes, however, are sewage effluent (outflow) and fertilizer runoff.

Most of a city's domestic waste and some industrial waste is washed down the sink, toilet, or drainage pipe and enters the municipal water system where it is treated. The degree of treatment depends on the facility. Even the most advanced facilities, which are few, still allow large quantities of nutrient-rich waste to flow into bodies of water for final dilution.

This sewage is rich in nitrogen, usually in the form of ammonia and nitrates, both of which exist in nature, but not in excessive amounts. The sewage in many parts of this country is also rich in phosphates, used in detergents. Phosphorus is an important nutrient found in limited amounts in aquatic ecosystems.

Even small amounts of phosphorus added to an aquatic ecosystem can have dramatic affects, resulting in an explosion of algae growth. In turn, this increase in algae causes a population explosion of bacteria that decompose the algae. Increased bacteria results in the loss of oxygen in the water and the decline of the ecosystem.

Project overview

Much of the concern about detergents centers on their effects on aquatic ecosystems. But what about land-based plants? This project investigates the effects of detergents on terrestrial plants, which often absorb the pollutants found in local ponds, lakes, and streams. Could this waste be used to encourage terrestrial plant growth? What would phosphate and enzyme detergents do to a terrestrial ecosystem? Would detergents help or hinder terrestrial plant growth?

This experiment investigates whether varying concentrations of phosphate and enzyme detergents will increase or decrease the growth of marigold plants.

Materials list

- 100 ml beaker
- ten seedling trays
- detergent that contains phosphates
- detergent that contains enzymes
- two packets of marigold seeds
- one or two grow lamps
- 25 lbs. of potting soil
- ruler with millimeter gradations
- microscope

Procedures

Prepare the seedling trays
Fill 10 seedling trays to the top with potting soil. Number the trays 1 through 10. In addition, refer to Fig. 15-1 and label each tray as fol-

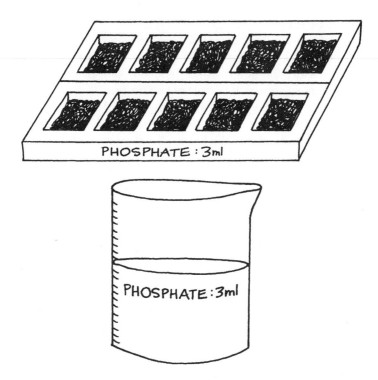

15-1 *Each group will have a seedling tray containing at least 10 plants and a beaker containing the proper watering solution.*

lows: trays 1 and 2—*Control*; trays 3 and 4—*Phosphate: 3ml*; trays 5 and 6—*Phosphate: 7ml*; trays 7 and 8—*Enzyme: 3ml*; and trays 9 and 10—*Enzyme: 7ml*.

Use your finger to make two holes in the soil of each cavity 1.5 cm deep (measure with the ruler). Place three seeds in each hole and cover them gently.

Prepare the watering solutions

Use a large beaker to hold the plain tap water that will be used on the control groups (1 and 2). Label this beaker *Control*. Put 3 mls of phosphate detergent and 25 mls of tap water in another beaker and label it *Phosphate: 3ml*. This will be used for trays 3 and 4. Put 7 mls of phosphate detergent and 25 mls of tap water in another beaker. Prepare similar beakers for the enzyme detergents with both 3 and 7 mls of detergent and 25 mls of water. Label these beakers appropriately.

Water and observe

Water the plants with a constant volume of water every third day (or more if necessary). After they are all watered, measure the plants. Use a ruler to measure the height of the plants. Rotate plants 180 degrees every 24 hours so they will not grow to one side.

Take notes about your observations. Record the date when the seedlings of each group appeared through the soil; how many leaves they each have; the color of the leaves; the diameters of the stems; etc.

After about six weeks, make observations and then remove typical samples of the leaves from each group. Look at the leaves under low power on a microscope and examine the microscopic structure of each plant.

Analysis

Were there differences between the control groups and the experimental groups? Were there differences between the four experimental groups? Did the detergents appear to help or hinder growth? After analyzing the gross structure, look at the microscopic structure. Was there any damage to the leaves in any of the groups? (See Fig. 15-2.) Look at the cell walls. Are they intact or has the cytoplasm leaked out?

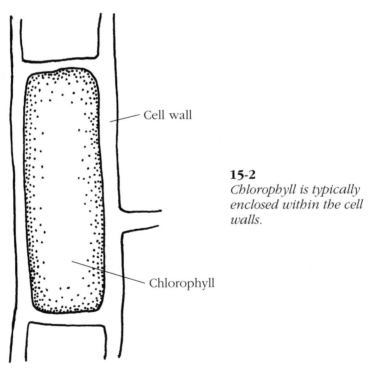

Cell wall

Chlorophyll

15-2
*Chlorophyll is typically
enclosed within the cell
walls.*

Going further

Continue by studying the soil in each pot. Compare its texture and structure. Has either detergent changed the soil physically or chemically?

For a completely different angle, perform a similar experiment but on emergent plants such as lily pads. If detergents accelerate plant growth in aquatic plants but reduce growth in terrestrial plants, what does it do to plants that live somewhere in between these extremes?

Suggested research

- Read about the impact of detergents on ecosystems and what has been and is being done about them.
- Investigate what manufacturers of these detergents are doing about the problem.

16

The hole in the ozone and terrestrial plants

What are the long-term effects of ultraviolet light on bean plants?

Background

Your home and auto air conditioners, refrigerator, and aerosol cans are the main culprits of ozone depletion. These items contain chlorofluorocarbons, more commonly called CFCs. Chlorofluorocarbons are thought to be responsible for eating a hole in the ozone layer in our atmosphere. This thin veil above the earth shields us and every living thing on our planet from excessive amounts of ultraviolet (UV) radiation. In small amounts, UV radiation causes little harm and even does some good. CFCs, however, destroy the molecules that help shield most of these UV rays from the earth.

Over the past few years, the amount of UV radiation hitting our planet has increased, raising concerns about the effect this increased exposure will have on us and other organisms.

Project overview

Not only is there concern about our health and the health of ecosystems, but what about our food crops? Are some of the staple food crops of the world being affected by increased levels of UV radiation?

This project investigates the effect of UV radiation exposure on the pinto bean, a major agricultural crop in some parts of the United States. If this plant is damaged by increased levels of UV, might the radiation cause harm to other crops, other organisms, and to us?

In this project, plants will be exposed to UV light. The health of the plants will be determined by noting their wet and dry weights, the percentage of germination, stem diameter, height, and chlorophyll absorption (optional). This project is divided into two parts. In the first, you will germinate the seeds and grow the plants. In the second, you will measure the resulting plants.

Materials list

- plant stands (the larger, the better; a three-tiered stand was used for the original experiment but any stand will work)
- room void of natural light
- paper towels
- UV lights (possibly available from your school or can be borrowed or purchased)
- incandescent light bulbs
- pinto beans
- distilled water
- timer switches to turn lights on and off
- potting soil
- plastic garden pots
- large graduated cylinder or other vessel to measure water
- ruler
- scale or balance
- calipers
- graph paper marked with square centimeters
- oven
- two fans (if not already attached to plant stand)

- thermometer
- black plastic trash bags
- plastic trays
- string

Procedures

The number of tiers and the number of fixtures within each tier will determine how many experimental groups you can grow at the same time. Modify this project to accommodate the available space in your plant stand(s). If you have multiple tiers or more than one stand available, make each stand or tier a separate group. These instructions assume you have available three tiers or stands to grow plants.

Set up each tier or stand with different lighting conditions. For example, place two UV bulbs in tier one, one UV bulb and one incandescent bulb in tier two, and two incandescent bulbs in tier three (see Fig. 16-1). Place one or more plastic trays in each tier. The trays will be used to first germinate the seeds, then hold the pots containing the seedlings.

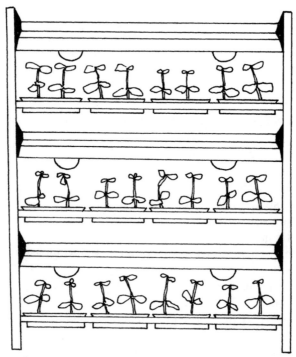

16-1 *If available, use a multi-tiered plant rack to create various combinations of UV and incandescent lighting.*

Growing the plants

Line the trays with paper towels and place about 25 pinto beans in the towels. Add water to each tray so the paper towels are soaked and a thin layer of standing water remains. Place all the lights in the stand on a timer and set it to a 12-hour light and 12-hour dark cycle. Also, hook up two small fans (they might be already attached to the stand) and leave them on at slow speed to continually circulate the air.

After about 11 days, observe the seeds. Record the number that germinated in each tray and the success of the germination. For example, do they have healthy roots or is there any browning present? After recording your observations about all the seeds, select the best seedlings to continue the project. Prepare the garden pots for the seedlings by placing 15 gs of potting soil in each pot. Place a seedling in each pot and cover with more soil. Add the same amount of soil to each pot.

Add 15 mls of water to each pot. Put the pots back in the same trays under the same lighting conditions in which they germinated. Water all the pots the same amount each day. This should be about 10 mls per day. Make observations each day after watering. Allow the plants to grow for 9 or 10 days before ending the growth period and beginning the quantitative analysis.

Taking measurements

You need to take five measurements to evaluate how UV radiation affected plant growth. First, measure the vertical height of the plants by holding the plant upright and pulling a string tight from the tip of the shoot to the ground (see Fig. 16-2). Next, measure the string with a ruler. Record this information for all the groups.

Second, obtain the plants' wet weights by carefully uprooting them. Be sure not to rip off any roots. Rinse off the soil from the roots and dry with paper toweling. Weigh each plant and record the data. Third, measure the thickness of the stem at the base with a vernier calipers.

Fourth, determine the area of the leaves by clipping a sample of leaves from each plant and placing it on graph paper. Trace the leaves onto the paper and count the number of squares in each leaf. Calculate the area of each leaf and assign an average to each plant.

Finally, determine the dry weight of each plant by taking half of the plants from each group and placing them in glass beakers. Place the beakers in a drying oven. When dry, weigh each beaker on a scale or balance. You can place five plants in each beaker and then determine the average for the group (figure in the beaker weight).

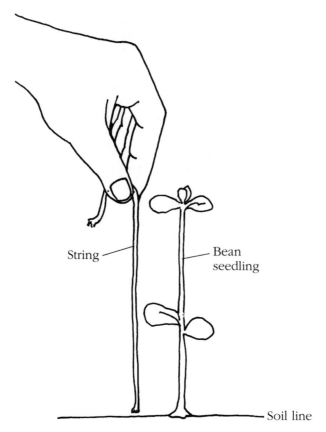

String —   — Bean
                                         seedling

                                      — Soil line

16-2 *Straighten the seedling and measure its length with a string.*

Analysis

Did UV radiation affect seed germination in any way? Did the degree of radiation make a difference? Was the percentage of germination different between groups? How about the five measurements of plant growth? Were there any differences in height, wet or dry weight, leaf area, or stem thickness? How about the root growth? Did any of the groups appear affected by the different levels of radiation?

Going further

Continue the project, but look for more detailed differences between the groups. For example, study the stomata on the leaves or look at root hairs under a dissecting scope. You could also continue the project to see if the seeds produced by plants exposed to UV radiation are as fertile as those from plants not exposed to the radiation.

Suggested research

- Investigate the current use and the latest legislation relating to CFCs. Look at both state and federal laws.
- Research studies about the effects of UV radiation on plant life of all sorts—from the algae to the forests.

Part 4

Plants and Plant Life

This section contains a diverse collection of projects that help you investigate the intricacies of plants and plant life. Chapter 17 studies which houseplants might remove indoor pollutants more quickly than others. Chapter 18 determines how a dry pond returns to life when refilled.

Chapter 19 looks for antibiotics from algae. Chapter 20 investigates whether physical contact can improve plant growth. Chapter 21 looks into plant growth hormones and how they control plants. Chapter 22 investigates whether ethylene gas affects the shelf life of fruits, and Chapter 23 looks into the association between plants and insects.

17

Indoor air pollution and houseplants

Which houseplants best clean the air?

Background

When you hear the phrase *air pollution*, you probably think of the air outside. Because we spend about 90% of our time indoors though, we should be concerned about the quality of indoor air as well. The Environmental Protection Agency considers indoor pollution one of the most misunderstood and understated of our environmental problems. Illnesses such as sick building syndrome and building-related illness are both recognized health problems caused by indoor pollution.

Two factors play major roles in indoor air pollution: tightly sealed buildings and increased use of synthetic materials in manufactured products like carpets and particleboard. Many of these materials give off toxic fumes such as formaldehyde, toluene, and xylene, which are then trapped inside the tightly sealed buildings.

Project overview

Recent studies have shown that some types of plants can help remove pollutants both from soil and air. This process is called *phytoremediation*. (*Bioremediation* refers to using both plants and animals to clean up pollutants.) Indoor plants have been shown to help clear air of many pollutants. Plants can act as filters, taking in polluted gases and releasing clean gases.

During photosynthesis, plants take in carbon dioxide and release oxygen and water vapor through their leaves and, sometimes, stems. This loss of water vapor is called *transpiration*. Transpiration can be used to indicate the amount of gases being exchanged between the plant and the atmosphere. If a link exists between the amount of gas passing through a plant and the amount of air cleaned by that plant, then we could select the best plants to clean the indoor air.

The purpose of this experiment is to see which houseplants have the highest transpiration rates under the same environmental conditions.

Materials list

- four different species of common houseplants (The more diverse the better. For example, look for plants from different original habitats; two specimens of each type.)
- sharp hobby knife
- analytical balance
- microscope
- microscope slides
- coverslips
- sandwich bags and ties (you cannot use resealable bags for this project)
- small adhesive labels
- 3-x-5-inch index cards
- ruler
- watch or clock
- refrigerator
- graph paper with 1 sq cm rules
- vernier calipers

Procedures

Initial observations

First, make microscopic observations of the leaves of each plant. Use a sharp hobby knife to slice a very thin section of the leaf epidermis and endodermis and the stem from each plant. Place the specimen on a microscope slide, add a drop of water, and cover with a coverslip. Look at slides for each plant. Look for the location of the stomata and record your observations. Also, look to see if stomata are located on both sides of the leaf and/or on the stems.

Experimental setup

Attach a label to each bag and identify it with a number. Use a balance or scale to measure and record the weight of a bag. Place a bag over a leaf and a small portion of the stem and seal with a tie. Make the tie tight, but not so tight as to harm the stem. Place a bag over one leaf on each plant (see Fig. 17-1). Place all the plants in the sunlight so the bagged leaf is directly facing the sun, and record the start time. Check the plants every half hour to ensure that each bagged leaf is still in direct sunlight.

Bring all the plants inside after six hours have elapsed. (You can adjust the elapsed time.) Immediately cut the leaf and stem off where the bag tie is located and place the bag, leaf, and stem in a refrigerator. The darkness and cold should stop any further transpiration. The cold should further help condense the transpired water vapor onto the inside of the bag.

Collecting data and determining transpiration rates

To determine the transpiration rate of each plant, you need three pieces of information: 1) the amount of water transpired, which we will call A; 2) the surface area of the plant that produced this water (includes the leaf and possibly the stem), which we will call B; and 3) the amount of time it took to transpire the water, which we will call C (see Fig. 17-2).

To find the amount of water transpired, remove a bag from the refrigerator and shake it gently so all of the condensed water goes to the bottom of the bag. Remove the tie from the bag, hold the stem,

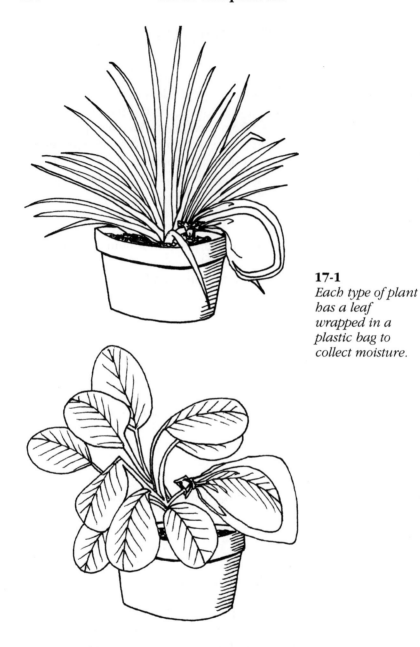

17-1
Each type of plant has a leaf wrapped in a plastic bag to collect moisture.

and gently shake the leaf to remove water still on the plant and collect it at the bottom of the bag. Wipe the leaves within the bag against the inside of the bag to remove any remaining water. All the water should now be collected at the bottom of the bag. Remove and save the leaf and stem in a separate, labeled bag.

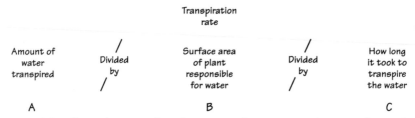

Amount of water transpired	/ Divided by /	Surface area of plant responsible for water	/ Divided by /	How long it took to transpire the water
A		B		C

17-2 *This formula is used to determine the transpiration rate for each plant.*

Fold up the bag (without the leaf and stem, but with the water collected at the bottom) and measure the weight on the balance. Subtract the original weight of the bag from the weight of the bag with the water. You now have the amount of water transpired by that specimen A, which is the first piece of information needed to calculate the transpiration rate.

Next, calculate the surface area of the plant that produced the water. The simplest way to do this is to trace the leaf on a piece of graph paper and count the number of squares and partial squares (see Fig. 17-3). Check with your sponsor for more accurate ways of calculating surface areas.

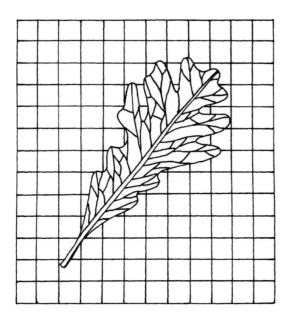

17-3
This is a simple way to determine the surface area of a leaf.

If during your initial observations of each plant's leaves and stems you recorded that stomata were found on both the bottom and the top of the leaves, you must multiply the surface area of each leaf, B, times two to account for the stomata on both sides of the leaf.

If you also noted during your initial observations that the plant had stomata on its stem, you must also add the surface area of the stem B. To do this, use a ruler to measure the length of stem that was enclosed in the bag and use the vernier calipers to measure the diameter of the stem. Then use the formula for determining the surface area of a cylinder (πdh, where d=diameter and h=height). Add this amount to B for the final surface area.

You are now ready to calculate the transpiration rate for that leaf. The transpiration rate is calculated by dividing the number of milligrams of water transpired A, by the surface area of the plant responsible for the transpiration B, by the amount of time it took to produce the water C, which we already know to be 6 hours. The formula therefore is: A/B/C.

Repeat this procedure of collecting data for the second leaf on each plant and determine the average of the two for that plant. Repeat this entire procedure for all the leaves on all the plants. Once you have calculated the transpiration rates for each type of plant, analyze your results.

Analysis

Did the transpiration rates vary greatly between the different types of plants? Does it appear that some types of plants exchange greater amounts of gases than others? If so, might the types of plants (and the number of plants) in your house or school make a difference in the quality of the indoor air?

Going further

Use your initial observations of the number of stomata and your final calculation of transpiration rates to see if there is a link between the two. Do more stomata necessarily mean a greater transpiration rate or do other factors play a role?

Suggested research

- Read the current literature about bioremediation. How are plants (and animals) being used to clean air and soil?
- Research the relationship between the transpiration rate and gas exchange. Is there a direct correlation?

18

Dried-up ponds

Can pond life survive without water?

Background

Have you ever seen a small pond or wet area once teeming with life completely dry up during a hot spell? You've probably observed that after a few days or weeks without water, the rains come and the life in the pond returns. Where did the plants and animals go during the dry spell?

Project overview

If a pond dries up completely and then weeks or months later refills with water, is it repopulated by organisms newly introduced to the pond or can some organisms survive droughts? This project attempts to determine if microscopic organisms can survive when a pond completely dries up or if a pond must be reinhabited.

During this project, you will simulate a pond becoming dry. You will then refill the "pond" with sterile water to be sure you are not introducing any organisms when the water is replaced. If organisms reappear without any outside intervention, we can assume microscopic organisms were present and waiting to repopulate the water.

This project contains two parts. In the first part, you will dehydrate the pond samples. In the second part, you will rehydrate the dried samples and make observations.

Materials list

- two samples of pond water that contain dirt and algae (preferably from two different ponds)
- two containers with lids
- enamel pan
- six petri dishes
- calcium chloride (probably available in your lab or from a scientific supply house)
- distilled water
- 500 ml flask
- autoclave (optional)
- microscope
- light and fixture
- eyedropper
- microscope slides and coverslips
- electric outlets
- desiccator vessel or a few drying U tubes (U tubes work much faster than the desiccator; either might be available in your school or from a scientific supply house.)
- field guide to microbial pond life (see recommendations at the end of this book)
- The items below are needed if you are using U tubes instead of the desiccator:
- cotton balls
- test tubes
- two-hole rubber stoppers
- rubber stoppers
- aquarium pump
- two right-angle glass rods
- rubber tubing

Procedures

Collect pond water

Sterilize the two collecting jars in an autoclave. (There are alternate ways of sterilizing jars without an autoclave. Speak with your sponsor about these techniques.) Collect two samples of pond water, preferably from different ponds. Be sure to include some dirt from the bottom—it can be along the water's edge. It would be best to include some greenish colored water because it contains algae.

Before proceeding, take a small sample from each collection jar and prepare a microscope slide. Use an eyedropper to place a drop of pond water on a microscope slide then cover it with a coverslip. Observe under the microscope and make detailed notes.

Take samples from the collection jars and place them in sterile petri dishes or test tubes. You can desiccate (dry out) the samples using one of two devices. If you have a desiccator, place the plates in the vessel as shown in Fig. 18-1.

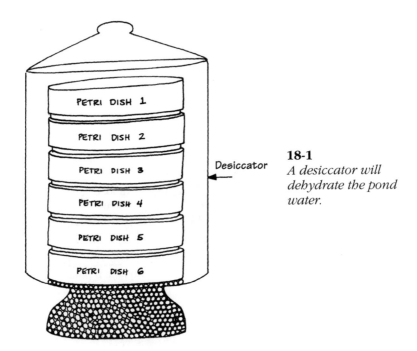

Desiccator

18-1
A desiccator will dehydrate the pond water.

Drying with a desiccator
First, sterilize six petri dishes. Then, thoroughly mix the collection jar contents and transfer 10 ml from each jar into a sterile petri dish. You'll have three petri dishes from each collection site.

Place the calcium chloride in the bottom of the desiccator. Microbes require oxygen, so do not seal the lid with petroleum jelly, as is usually done. This process will take many days. For a faster method, use a U tube.

Drying with a U tube
If you must proceed more rapidly, you can use a U tube. The disadvantage of this method is that you'll need one U tube for each sample to be desiccated. If you are using U tubes, they must first be

sterilized. Once sterilized, thoroughly mix the pond water samples in the collection jar and transfer 10 ml from each jar into a sterile test tube. You'll have three test tubes from each collection site.

Set up the U tubes as seen in Fig. 18-2. Plug the test tube containing the sample with a two-hole stopper. Insert right-angle glass tubes into both of these holes. Attach one of these right angle tubes to the U tube nipple with rubber tubing, as seen in the figure. Stuff the end of the rubber tube with cotton to keep the granules from entering the tubing. Fill the U tube with calcium chloride granules. Plug both ends of the U tube with rubber stoppers. Attach a rubber tube to the other U tube nipple. Stuff it with cotton. Attach this tube to an aquarium pump, and plug the pump into an outlet.

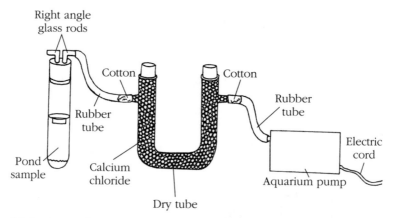

18-2 *A U tube apparatus will dehydrate the pond water more quickly than a desiccator.*

The pump blows air through the U tube where it is thoroughly dried. The dry air passes through the test tube sample and carries away the moisture quite rapidly.

Rehydrate and observe

After the water has been removed, place the petri dishes or test tubes in a dry room where they will get natural light. (Plug the test tubes with cotton.) After 48 hours, take the first test tube or petri dish from each pond sample and rehydrate it with sterile water by adding 10 milliliters of sterile water to the petri dish or test tube. If you are using a test tube, it must remain plugged with cotton.

Take a sample and place it on a microscope slide. Add a cover-slip and look at the sample under the microscope. Use a field guide to microbial pond life to help you identify what you see. Continue taking samples and making observations every 10 minutes. Repeat the same procedure for the first test tube or petri dish from the other pond sample. Take detailed notes and compare them with the notes you wrote when you first collected the samples.

Leave the other four test tubes or petri dishes (two sets of two from each pond) for another five days, then repeat your observations. Leave the final two tubes or plates for one month, then repeat your observations for the last time.

Analysis

What types of pond life did you find when you first collected the pond water samples? Did you find protists, rotifers, and/or green algae? After the water was dried and rehydrated, what organisms did you find in the water, if any? Did the pond life contain all the organisms found in the original samples, or just a few?

After one week and one month of remaining in a dry state, did the pond life return when the samples were rehydrated? After the water was replaced, did you see any organisms or unique forms that were not present in the original samples? What are they? Use your field guide to help identify what you see.

Going further

Will the environment in which the dehydrated pond life is held affect the outcome of this project? For example, hold the dehydrated samples in an environment that continually receives light or receives no light. Try an environment that reaches 100°C or freezes.

Try to perform a similar experiment, but do a small field study. Modify this project to use an actual pond that has dried up.

Suggested research

- Investigate the life cycles of the organisms you found in the water after they were dehydrated. How do they survive?
- Find out how higher forms of plant life recolonize a pond after it dries out. Do emergent plants such as water lilies immediately return to a refilled pond?

19

Using algae for medicinal purposes

Does algae have any medicinal qualities?

Background

Algae has been used as a medicine for centuries. Mariners once used marine algae as a medicine. They wrapped wounds in bandages made of kelp (a seaweed). These mariner and other folk remedies have received renewed interest in recent years. Scientists are studying the antimicrobial qualities of many species of algae.

Kelp and seaweeds are brown algae (see Fig. 19-1). Brown algae are all multicellular and can grow quite large. Some look like aquatic plants with root systems and blades that resemble leaves. The cells of brown algae contain chlorophyll, responsible for photosynthesis, but their golden-brown pigment usually masks all other colors, including green.

Project overview

If you live near the ocean, you've probably seen seaweed or kelp washed on shore. Powdered kelp is sold in health food stores and

116

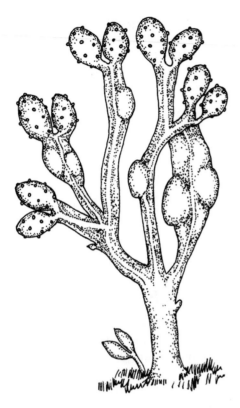

19-1
Kelp is a large brown algae that was used by mariners as a salve to heal wounds.

used as a health supplement. This investigation explores whether seaweed or kelp found along the shore or sold in the store actually have antimicrobial qualities. Does seaweed or kelp kill bacteria?

Materials list

- seaweed or kelp (collect your own or use powdered kelp purchased from a health food store)
- algae identification manual (if you are collecting your own)
- large plastic bags (resealable type)
- scissors or scalpel
- pipette
- paper towels
- screw-cap vials
- balance or scale
- sterile antibiotic disks (from a scientific supply house)
- spatula
- mortar and pestle
- cultures of *E. coli* or other nonpathogenic, gram-negative

bacteria on at least three tryptic soy agar plates (from a
scientific supply house; can be purchased or prepared)
- cultures of *Bacillus subtilis* or other nonpathogenic, gram-
  positive bacteria on at least three tryptic soy agar plates (from
  a scientific supply house)
- sterile distilled water
- cotton swabs
- tweezers or eyedropper
- pot
- refrigerator
- flask
- adhesive tape
- incubator
- petri dishes
- ruler

Procedures

You can either collect your own algae or use powdered kelp that
you've purchased. Sterile (aseptic) technique must be used throughout this project. Speak with your sponsor about these techniques as
you discuss the project.

Collecting and preparing seaweed
First, study an identification guide so you know what you are looking
for at the beach. Speak with your sponsor about the various species
that might be found in your location. Use large resealable plastic bags
to collect a few handfuls of the algae. Bring the bags back to the lab
and dry them thoroughly with paper towels.

Cut off and weigh 25 g of algae. Place this into the mortar and
add 5 ml of sterile distilled water. Grind thoroughly until a soupy liquid remains. (Alternately, you could blend the algae.) Pour the liquid
into a screw-cap tube for temporary storage.

Preparing powdered kelp
If you are using powdered kelp instead of fresh specimens, weigh out
20 g of the powder and place it in the mortar. Add 5 ml of distilled
sterile water and mix thoroughly. Pour this liquid into a screw-cap
tube for temporary storage.

Preparing the plates
Using sterile technique, saturate a sterile antibiotic disk with the seaweed or kelp liquid you created earlier, and place it in one of the *E.*

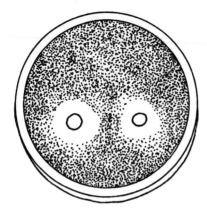

19-2
Use the seaweed to create antibiotic disks.

coli culture plates as seen in Fig. 19-2. Next, place a second saturated disc in the other half of the plate, as seen in Fig 19-2. Use a sterile pipette or eyedropper and tweezers to do this.

Repeat this process with two other plates so there are three plates in this group. Repeat the process with the three *Bacillus subtilis* plates. Seal all the plates shut with adhesive tape. Be sure to label all the plates. You'll have two groups of three plates with two discs in each.

Place all the plates in an incubator at 37°C for 48 hours. After this time, remove the plates from the incubator. Use a millimeter ruler to measure the *zone of inhibition* around each disc. This is the area around the disc in which no bacteria colonies grow. Record your observations. When finished, discuss with your sponsor the proper way to dispose of these plates.

Analysis

After measuring the zones of inhibition for each plate, average those for each group. Did the algae have any antibacterial qualities? If so, does it resist one type of bacteria more than the other? Did mariners of long ago have a good idea?

Going further

Perform a similar experiment, but speak with your sponsor about making an extract of the seaweed instead of simply grinding it up. You can also compare different concentrations of the extract and observe the effects. If you live in an area where seaweeds and kelps are common, try different types. Are any superior to others?

Suggested research

- Research old folk medicine uses of seaweeds and other algae. Were they an important part of early medicine?
- Research modern day medicinal use of seaweeds and other algae; are they making a comeback?

20

Stimulating plant growth

Will physically stimulating plants increase plant growth?

Background

Some gardeners claim that talking to plants improves plant growth. If true, the ramifications could be enormous. Crop yields could be improved by creating machines that play recorded music to vast fields of wheat and corn. This might sound farfetched, but there is some evidence that certain types of stimulation can affect the growth of some plants.

Project overview

In nature, plants are moved by wind and struck by rain, but greenhouse plants don't get this natural stimulation. If naturally stimulated plants grow better than those grown in greenhouses, then understanding the relationship between stimulation and growth could improve plant growth in greenhouses. Some research shows that touch results in shorter plants. Other research shows that touching plants induces the release of ethylene gas, resulting in accelerated growth.

Can artificially induced stimuli such as wind and rain improve the growth of Swedish Ivy (*Plectrantheus australis*) in a greenhouse environment? Will either of these stimuli produce a healthier plant?

Materials list

- access to a greenhouse (This can be a large commercial greenhouse or a small, temporary greenhouse built for this experiment. You might be able to borrow space in a greenhouse for this project.)
- forty 15-cm cuttings of Swedish Ivy
- rooting medium (can be purchased or made from two parts peat moss and one part sharp sand)
- potting soil (mix two parts of a good quality potting soil with one part peat moss and one part sand)
- twenty 1-gal clear plastic bags
- large opaque plastic sheets (large plastic garbage bags will work fine)
- plant fertilizer (15-30-15)
- spray bottle
- pruning shears
- distilled water
- four plant (seedling) trays that can hold 10 plants each
- soaker trays to retain water (enough to hold all the plant trays)
- feather duster
- house fan
- wood rods attached to a base so they stand upright (see Fig. 20-2)
- transparent plastic wrap
- balance or electronic scale
- micrometer
- rubber bands
- automatic electric timers
- garden hose

Procedures

Root the plants
During the first part of the project, you must prepare a group of similar plant cuttings for the control and experimental groups. Once the

cuttings have taken root, they will be divided into groups and the experiment can begin.

To prepare the plants, place 10 cms of the rooting medium into each of the clear plastic bags. Take 40 15-cm cuttings from the ivy plants. Slice the plants just below a leaf joint and strip the bottom leaf. Place each cutting 8 centimeters deep into the potting soil within the bags. Put three cuttings into each bag (see Fig. 20-1). Press down on the potting mixture to make it firm enough to support the plants upright. Be sure the three cuttings are not touching one another.

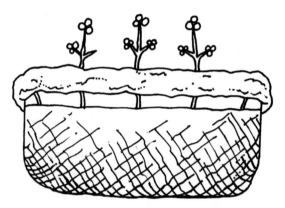

20-1
Each bag will contain three cuttings.

Spray the plants within each bag just enough to wet them, then pull the opening of the bag together and blow air into the bag so it becomes inflated. Seal the bag tightly with a knot and rubber band. Keep all the bags in the greenhouse so they get plenty of light and remain warm. After one week, open up the bags and check the roots. They should be about 2.5 cms long. If they are too short, re-close the bag and wait another few days.

Once all the roots have attained the proper length, begin rolling down the sides of the bags a little each day to accustom the plants to the room temperature. This process should last a few more days. The plants are now ready for potting. Fill the plant trays with the potting soil mixture and transplant 10 of the rooted cuttings into each of the four trays.

The trays must be separated with opaque plastic sheets about 1 m high, as shown in Fig. 20-2. You can use wood rods, PVC pipes, or anything that can be attached to a base to stand upright and support plastic bags. Attach the plastic sheets to this frame to act as dividers. All the trays must receive the same amount of light and water.

Next, prepare the plant food by mixing 1 ml of food for every 4 liters of distilled water. You'll need 1 liter for each tray every other

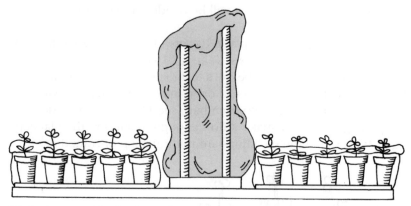

20-2 *Prop up black plastic bag dividers to keep the groups separated from each other.*

week. The plants must be fed this solution every other week. You must also have enough plain distilled water to water all the plants once every other week. When feeding and watering the plants, pour the liquid into the soaker trays that contain the plant trays to keep the water from contacting with the plants, which is one of the experimental factors.

The exact amount of food and water will vary depending on the conditions in the greenhouse. Adjust accordingly, but always keep the amount consistent between all groups and document your procedures. Water (with distilled water) and feed the plants (with the food solution) on alternate weeks (adjust as needed).

Apply stimuli

The four trays can now be divided into two project groups: water stimulation and air stimulation. Both groups contain two trays. One tray is a control and the other is exposed to the appropriate stimuli. Label each group and its trays. Now, set up the appropriate stimulus apparatus for each group.

For the air stimulation group, place a fan 60 cms away from the first tray. Leave the fan on for three hours every day. Timers will make this easier to manage. The second tray is the control for this group and should receive no air movement at all.

For the water stimulation group, lay strips of plastic sheeting on the two trays to cover the soil. Crisscross these strips to create layers that will cause dripping water to drain off the strips and not be absorbed into the soil. You don't want the stimulus water to be absorbed into the soil because this would add another variable.

Use a garden hose to spray water on one of the trays in this group for two minutes twice a day. Leave the second tray as a control, receiving no water stimulation. For consistency's sake, it too should have the plastic sheeting.

Continue watering, feeding, and applying the appropriate stimuli to each group over a six-week period. Keep diligent notes each day about what was done and when. Also, make general observations about the health of the plants in each group. Don't take any actual measurements because this would act as a stimulus. After six weeks, you are ready to take the final measurements to determine how the groups compare.

Analysis

Before taking measurements, record your observations about the overall appearance of all the plants, then measure the shoot length for each plant in all of the trays. Measure the shoot diameter. Use a micrometer to measure the average leaf thickness. Gently remove the plants from the soil and measure the root length. Clean the soil from the roots and measure the weight of the entire plant—shoots and roots. After the plants have dried, weigh the entire plant again.

Once you have collected the raw data, plot a graph for each of the trays. How did the trays within each group compare? Did the plants in the experimental trays grow better than the controls? Did the stimulation appear to help or hinder plant growth? Did stimulation have no effect on the plants? Once you analyze the data within each group, compare the groups. Did one form of stimulation result in more growth than another stimulation? Does it appear that some forms of stimulation improved the growth of greenhouse plants?

Going further

Based on your results from this project, continue testing additional amounts of stimulation. For example, if you found that water stimulation for two minutes, twice each day resulted in improved growth, set up the experiment to test two minutes of stimulation three to six times per day. Is there a point of diminishing returns? You can also study whether there is a synergistic effect when both stimuli are applied together.

Suggested research

- Study the latest research developments in this field.
- Investigate how any positive results (improved growth due to stimulation) could be applied commercially. Would it be economically practical?

21

Plant growth regulators

Can you make a plant grow straight?

Background

Scientists have discovered many hormones in plants that regulate their growth. Some of these substances have useful applications. Gibberelins and auxins are two substances used in state-of-the-art herbicides. Because these substances control a plant's growth, they can be manipulated to kill unwanted plants, such as weeds. For example, some plant hormones are sprayed on plants to make them grow so rapidly that they collapse on themselves and die.

One advantage of using growth hormones is that they are specific to a single type of plant, as opposed to most chemical herbicides, which kill many types of plants. The use of plant growth hormones has expanded to other areas besides plant control. For example, agriculturists have researched the use of growth hormones to manipulate and improve commercially grown plants.

Project overview

Plants bend toward light, due in part to a phytohormone called *indole-3-acetic acid* (IAA). IAA causes plant cells to elongate. If IAA exists throughout a plant stem, all the cells elongate and the plant grows straight up. However, experiments have shown that light causes IAA to degrade, meaning those cells facing the light will no longer elongate. If the cells facing the light don't grow, but those on the opposite side of the light continue to grow (they still have active IAA), the stem will bend toward the light.

Some studies have shown that certain growth-regulating hormones can interfere with the normal metabolism of IAA. If a substance could be found that would prevent a plant from bending toward the light, it might have commercial applications. For example, houseplants would remain straight without having to continually turn them to face a window.

This project uses a substance called *scopoletin*, which is believed to inhibit the degradation of IAA by light, and results in a straight-growing plant regardless of the location of the light. The original project on which this project was based had inconclusive results. It is, however, an excellent experiment and should be considered a model from which you can create your own investigation. Consider performing a similar experiment using varying amounts of scopoletin or reading about other growth regulatory substances and using them in a similar experiment. Speak with your advisor about the possibilities.

Materials list

- 100 g lanolin paste (available from a scientific supply house)
- 10 mg scopoletin (available from a chemical supply house)
- small amount of denatured ethyl alcohol (from a scientific supply house)
- two 250-ml glass beakers
- 1000 ml glass beaker
- stirring rods
- heating plate
- analytical balance
- spatula
- aluminum foil
- paper towels
- thirty plastic pots (for small seedlings)
- potting soil
- garden shovel
- oat (*Avena sativa*) seeds (available from a supply house or in loose bushels from an organic supermarket)
- scalpel
- flat wooden toothpicks
- grow lamps

- index cards
- protractor
- cm ruler

Procedures

Preparing the seedlings

Germinate the oat seeds by placing them between two layers of damp paper towels for two to three days. Keep the towels damp throughout, but not soaked. Prepare the pots by filling them with soil. After the seeds have germinated, transplant them into the pots. Insert them 1 cm deep in the soil. Place only one plant in each pot. Allow the seedlings to grow for four to five days. Water, light, and other environmental factors should be kept constant for all the plants.

Preparing the scopoletin paste

Weigh out 100 g of lanolin paste in a 250 ml beaker. Use a spatula to transfer the lanolin because it is very thick. Dissolve 5 mg or less of scopoletin in 0.2 ml of denatured ethyl alcohol in another 250 ml beaker. Use a stirring rod to thoroughly dissolve the crystalline powder.

Double boiler

Place the 250 ml glass beaker containing the lanolin in a 1000 ml glass beaker. Add enough water to the 1000 ml beaker so the waterline reaches just above the level of the lanolin in the other beaker. Place the large beaker on a hot plate and slowly heat the lanolin at a medium temperature until it liquefies (see Fig. 21-1).

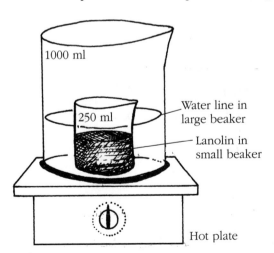

1000 ml

250 ml

Water line in large beaker

Lanolin in small beaker

Hot plate

21-1
The lanolin paste is placed in the small beaker which is placed in the large beaker that contains water, creating a double boiler.

Use tongs to remove the large beaker from the hot plate and the small beaker from the large beaker, then pour the scopoletin and ethyl alcohol solution prepared earlier into the beaker of lanolin paste. Mix thoroughly using a stirring rod. Cover this beaker with tin foil, label it, and refrigerate until needed.

Preparing the plants
You now have a beaker containing the experimental paste and at least 30 five-day-old seedlings. Because the tip of the stem is where IAA is produced, remove the tips from all of the stems. This prevents the continuation of IAA production and limits it to the IAA already present in the stems. Use a ruler to mark the seedling 4 mls from the top. Hold the seedling gently in place with one hand and use a scalpel to cut off the top 4 mls of stem. (Be sure to have your sponsor help you with this procedure.) Measure the height of the remaining stem and record the data. Repeat this procedure with all of the plants.

Measuring the plant stem curve
Next, measure the initial curve of the stem so it can be compared with the final curve of the plant after growth. To do this, cut a file card narrow enough so that it fits into the pot to the soil line. Mark a dot, A, in the middle of the bottom edge of the card and draw a vertical line perpendicular to the soil, B (see Fig. 21-2).

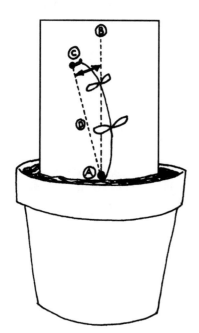

21-2
The file card is used to measure the angle of the stem curvature, as described in the Procedures section.

Hold the card alongside the plant with dot A located where the stem comes out of the soil, as seen in the figure. Hold the card so vertical line B is perpendicular to the soil. Mark with a dot on the card the location of the end of the stem, C. Remove the card from the plant and use a ruler to draw a line from dot C (the end of the stem) to dot A (the location of the stem coming out of the soil) to create line D. Then use a protractor to measure the angle between lines B and D. This is the curvature of the plant at the beginning of the project.

Applying the growth regulator

Now that you know the original curvature of the plant, you can begin the experiment. Separate the seedlings into three groups. One is the control, which receives no application; another is group one, to which you will apply the paste to the side of the stem facing the light; and the final group, which will receive paste on the side opposite the light. There should be at least 10 plants in each group, but preferably more.

Remove the beaker containing the scopoletin paste from the refrigerator and liquefy it, following the previous instructions regarding the double boiler. Once the paste is liquid, dip a flat toothpick into the solution and apply the paste to the entire length of one side of each of the 20 experimental plants.

Immediately after the application is complete, place all of the plants the same distance from grow lamps. Experimental group one should have the side with the paste application *facing* the light. Group two should have the side with the paste application facing *away* from light. All three groups (including the control group) must receive the same amount of light and be kept under similar environmental conditions. Be sure the entire length of all the stems is in the direct light. This might mean cutting a portion of the pot away. Expose the plants to 10 hours of continuous light.

Observations

After 10 hours, make general observations about the health of the plants and their features. Then repeat the procedures for measuring the plant stem curve, as previously described. This will be the final curvature for each plant. Record the results alongside the initial curvature measurements taken earlier.

Analysis

Compare the change in the stem curve for all the plants, then compare the three groups. The control group should have naturally curved toward light. What happened with the two experimental groups? Was there any difference between the two experimental groups and/or the control? What was the effect of the scopoletin on either side of the stem.

Going further

As mentioned in the "Project overview" section, the original project showed inconclusive results. Might the concentration of scopoletin make a difference? Could this project be revised to test a range of concentrations? Devise a similar project to test growth regulators other than scopoletin.

Suggested research

- Read about plant hormones, including auxins and gibberelins. What are they used for and how?
- Investigate cell elongation in plants. What research has been done on this subject?

22

Ethylene gas and plant growth

Does ethylene gas affect plant growth?

Background

One rotten apple spoils the barrel. This cliché has lingered in our language for decades, but is it true? Can one rotten apple really accelerate the rotting of other apples in the same bushel?

Ripening apples emit ethylene gas. This gas helps ripen the fruit. Ethylene gas is used commercially to ripen harvested green fruits such as mangoes, honeydews, and bananas. To induce natural ethylene ripening, farmers sometimes wrap pears or peaches in paper, which keeps the gas from escaping.

Project overview

This project proceeds with the informal hypothesis that one rotten apple can spoil other apples. This experiment was designed to test the effects of ethylene gas on beans, bean sprouts, and young bean plants. Does ethylene gas, which is produced naturally by these plants, hasten the growth process within beans, bean plant sprouts, and young bean plants?

This project is divided into three parts. In the first, you will test the effects of gases emitted by an apple on a bean (seed). In the second part, you will see the effect of this gas on bean sprouts, and the third part tests the effects on young plants.

Materials list

- fresh bag of pinto beans
- twelve apples (similar shape and size)
- twenty-four garden racks (the type used to hold up tomato plants)
- twelve flower pots, sized to accommodate the racks
- potting soil for all the pots
- plastic wrap (the kind painters use to protect furniture)
- twenty-four small paper plates
- seedling tray
- camera (optional)

Procedures

Expose bean seeds

Construct a series of tomato racks covered in plastic wrap, as seen in Fig. 22-1. The plastic racks, called hoods, look similar to plastic lamp shades. The hoods should capture gases emitted by the apples. Tuck the wrap beneath the bottom of the racks. The hood should become engulfed in gases, and can then be used to expose plants to the gas.

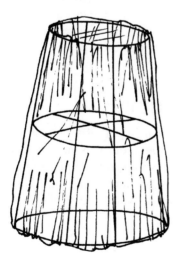

22-1
The hoods look something like lamp shades.

First, test the effects of ethylene gas on beans (seeds). Take four beans and place them on a small paper plate with an apple. Place the plate with the beans and apple under a hood for two weeks. Label the hood: *Beans/Apple/1*. Assemble two more hoods with beans and apples, numbered 2 and 3. Then construct three more with hoods but leave out the apples. This is the control group. Label the control *Beans/1* through *Beans/3*, as seen Fig. 22-2. You now have three experimental hoods and three controls.

After two weeks of exposure to the apple, remove the beans from the hoods and plant them in separate pots about 2 cms deep in the soil. Wait for the beans to sprout and grow. Water each bean with 60 mls of water each day. Take photographs each week as you collect data. Measure the sprout height each day and record the date the sprouts break through the soil, the date the cotyledons fall off, the number of leaves, and the general health of the plants.

Expose bean sprouts

Plant about 25 beans 2 cms deep in seedling trays, water daily, and wait for them to sprout. Once sprouted, select six similar sprouts and plant each in its own small pot.

Place one sprout pot on a plate with an apple and place it under a hood. Repeat this with two more bean sprouts. Label the pots *Sprouts/Apple/1* through 3 (see Fig. 22-2). Place the remaining three sprout pots under separate hoods but include no apples. Label these *Sprouts/1* through 3, as seen in the figure. Keep the remaining sprouts, because they'll be used in the last part of this project.

Water the sprouts daily with 60 mls of water. The apples will completely rot after about 10 days, so replace them with fresh ones. Make observations each day as with the bean seeds and take photographs weekly. Concentrate on the number and color of the leaves.

Expose bean plants

Transplant six seedlings from the seedling tray (planted earlier) into six pots. Wait for these seedlings to grow 10 cms tall, then place three of them under separate hoods, each with an apple. Do the same for three controls but include no apples. Water the plants daily with 60 mls of water. Observe daily and take photographs weekly.

Analysis

For Part One, how long did it take for the beans to sprout through? Did one group appear sooner? Was there a difference in growth pat-

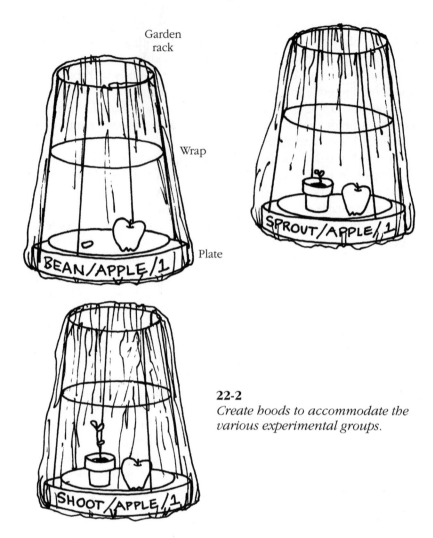

Garden rack

Wrap

Plate

BEAN/APPLE/1

SPROUT/APPLE/1

SHOOT/APPLE/1

22-2
Create hoods to accommodate the various experimental groups.

terns between the experimental and control groups? Might a gas emitted by the apple have caused differences between these groups?

For Parts Two and Three, did the experimental groups of sprouts and shoots grow differently from the controls? Were any differences beneficial or harmful to the growth of the plants? Did any unusual types of growth appear?

Compare all three parts of the experiment. Does the presence of the apple have a beneficial or harmful effect on the development and growth of bean plants?

Going further

During this project, we assumed that ethylene gas was produced by the apple. Modify the experiment to determine what type of gas and how much of that gas is emitted by the apple and how much is trapped beneath the hood.

Devise an experiment to specifically test the phrase "one rotten apple spoils the barrel." See if one rotting apple will ripen other, less mature apples when they are packaged together.

Suggested research

- Research how food packagers use ethylene gas.
- Investigate the effects of ethylene gas besides ripening. What other roles does it play?
- Look into other substances produced by plants that affect their development.

23

Plant and insect associations

How do insects use plants for food and protection?

Background

Plants are not only food to many types of animals, but they are also home to many organisms, especially insects. Insects often live in close association with plants. Some insects with the most interesting relationships to plants are leaf miners, leaf rollers, and gall producers (see Fig. 23-1).

Leaf miners create narrow tunnels (mines) within plant leaves. An adult insect lays an egg within the leaf. The immature insect emerges from its egg to live between the top and bottom surfaces of the leaf. It feeds within the leaf and, in doing so, creates small but visible mines in the leaf. As the insect grows, the mine gets wider. The insect continues its life cycle within the leaf until the adult burrows its way out.

You can easily see this tunneling when looking at an affected leaf. You can even see the tunnel getting wider as the larva grows. The narrowest portion of the tunnel is where the egg was laid. The widest portion of the tunnel is where the adult emerged from the plant.

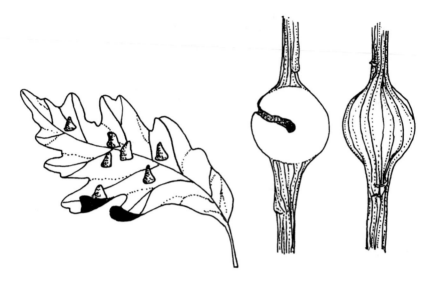

23-1 *Galls are created by an interesting association between plants and insects.*

Galls are deformities in plants. Some look like small, odd growths protruding from leaves or stems, while others are large, round growths that almost look as if they are part of the natural plant. Galls, however, are not normal plant growths. Galls are caused by plant diseases, worms, or most often, insects. Insects produce a substance that causes plants to produce growths (the galls), which the insects use for protection.

The leaf roller uses a leaf for protection as it matures. It rolls the leaf up into a cylinder around its body.

Project overview

This project investigates two areas. First, how common are these plant structures? If you were to survey the plants in a plot of land, what percentage of the plants in the area or what percentage of a plant contains leaf miner, rollers, or galls? The second part investigates the type and extent of damage insects can cause to leaves. What happens to the cells of a leaf when a leaf miner feeds through it? How does the presence of galls affect plant cells? Is the leaf or stem killed by this intrusion?

Materials list

- field guide to identify leaf mining, rolling, and gall damage
- dissecting microscope
- compound microscope
- scalpel
- forceps
- plastic bags for collecting
- hand lens or magnifying glass

Procedures

Search for damage

From summer to early fall, look for plants containing galls, leaf mining, and leaf rolling damage. Look on the leaves and stems of shrubs, trees, and other plants for these structures. A walk in the woods would probably yield the best results. Quantify the percentage of all the plants and parts of each plant that have damage. For example, what percentage of all the oak tree saplings in a given area have galls, or what percentage of all the leaves on a plant have leaf mining damage? You'll have to make many observations to obtain large-enough samples.

Collect and study samples

Collect at least 10 examples of damage. Do this by cutting off the small portion of the plant containing the damage and placing it in a plastic resealable bag. Bring the bags back to the lab and use your field guide to help you identify the types of damage. Look at the damage using the dissecting microscope first. Look at the gross structure of the damage to the leaf or stem. Before dissecting the damage, take notes and make sketches of your observations.

Once you have studied the external structures, dissect each specimen and study the internal structure of the plant damage and search for the insects that caused the damage. Cut galls open with a scalpel. First, look for insect larvae, and try to identify them. Proceed by carefully cutting the gall into smaller pieces and studying the plant cells. Look at the cells first under the dissecting scope, then make slides and look at them under the compound microscope. Look for differences in the size and shapes of the cells.

Leaf miners are usually very small and might be hard if not impossible to locate. Use the microscope or magnifying glass to look at the end of the widest portion of the mine. Is there a small hole at the end? If so, this is the emergence hole where the adult insect left the leaf. It could be on the top, bottom, or even the edge of the leaf. Use the dissecting scope first and then the compound microscope to study the cells in the damaged area. Take notes and make sketches of all your observations.

To study the leaf roller, first examine what the insect did to the leaf. How did it keep the leaf rolled up like a cigar? Then unroll the leaf using forceps and the scalpel. Tease the holding material apart to unravel the leaf. What is inside? Try to identify the insect. Observe the structure of the leaf.

Analysis

Are these plant/insect relationships common where you live? Is a large or small proportion of the plant population affected by these intruders? Does the damage appear to harm the plant to any significant degree? What would happen if the plants died with the insects in them?

How do the plant cells appear to be affected in each type of damage? What has happened to the cells in a leaf that has been mined or grown into a gall? What type of destruction does the leaf miner do within the leaf? What has happened to a plant's cells that make it grow abnormally into galls?

Going further

Follow the development of a gall or a leaf miner. The best time to do this is the late spring. Identify a tree, for example, where you found old gall growths on decaying leaves or stems. Begin your observations at the first site of the damage. Take samples every week and continue until the growth is complete. Study the plant pathology of the damage as it proceeds.

Suggested research

- Read more about the plant pathology of gall producers and leaf miners. How does the intruder select the host plant? What stimulates the plant to produce the gall?
- Study the co-evolution of plants and insects.

Appendix

Using metrics

Most science fairs require all measurements be taken using the metric system as opposed to English units. Meters and grams, which are based on powers of 10, are far easier to use during your experimentation than feet and pounds.

You can convert English units into metric units if need be, but it is easier to simply begin with metric units. If you are using school equipment such as flasks or cylinders, check the graduations to see if any have metric units. If you are purchasing your glassware (or plasticware), order metric graduations.

Note that when English measurements are used in this book, it is to correspond with the most popular packaging of an item. For example, most lumberyards measure in feet and would be puzzled if you ordered in metric units.

Conversions from English units to metric units are given as follows, along with their abbreviations as used in this book. All conversions are approximations.

Length
1 inch (in) = 2.54 centimeters (cm)
1 foot (ft) = 30 cm
1 yard (yd) = 0.90 meters (m)
1 mile (mi) = 1.6 kilometers (km)

Volume
1 teaspoon (tsp) = 5 milliliters (ml)
1 tablespoon (tbsp) = 15 ml
1 fluid ounce (fl oz) = 30 ml
1 cup (c) = 0.24 liters (l)

1 pint (pt) = 0.47 l
1 quart (qt) = 0.95 l
1 gallon (gal) = 3.80 l

Mass
1 ounce (oz) = 28.00 grams (g)
1 pound (lb) = 0.45 kilograms (kg)

Temperature
32 degrees Fahrenheit (F) = 0 degrees Celsius (C)
212 degrees F = 100 degrees C

Glossary

abscission The dropping of leaves, flowers, or fruit from a plant.

abstract A brief written overview that describes your project, usually less than 250 words and often required at science fairs.

accessory pigment A pigment, other than chlorophyll, that captures light energy and transfers it to chlorophyll.

aerobe An organism that requires oxygen to survive.

algae Simple photosynthetic plants. They might be one-celled, microscopic organisms or live in large macroscopic colonies. They are found in almost all aquatic habitats. (Excludes blue-green algae.)

anaerobe Organisms that can live in the absence of oxygen.

angiosperm A group of plants whose seeds are found within a mature ovary (fruit).

annual A plant whose entire life cycle is accomplished in a single growing season.

anther The pollen-bearing portion of the stamen.

autotroph An organism that produces its own food (by photosynthesis using the sun or from inorganic chemicals). Also called a *producer.*

auxin A group of plant growth hormones.

backboard The vertical, self-supporting panel used in a science fair display. The board usually displays the problem, hypothesis, photos of the apparatus used, organisms, and other important aspects of the project, as well as analyzed data in the form of charts and tables. Most fairs have size limitations for backboards.

berry A fleshy fruit that contains an ovary wall and at least one carpel and seed; examples are: grapes, tomatoes, and bananas.

biocontrol The use of organisms to control pests, also called biological control.

bryophytes Nonvascular, terrestrial plants; for example, mosses.

bulb An underground food storage organ of a plant.

cell The basic unit of life. Cells are bags containing a liquid interior (the cytoplasm). Enclosed are organelles and genetic material.

The bag itself is the cell membrane. Organisms are either unicellular (e.g., protists) or multicellular (e.g., humans).

cellulose This carbohydrate is the primary component of the cell wall in most plants. It is composed of glucose molecules.

chlorophyll The green pigment of plant cells responsible for capturing radiant energy during photosynthesis.

chloroplast An organelle in the cells of green plants that contain chlorophyll.

community All the populations (plants and animals) living within a specified area.

compound leaf A leaf with blades divided into separate leaflets.

consumer An organism that must consume (eat) its food as opposed to making its food. Also called *heterotrophs*.

control group A test group in an experiment that provides a baseline for comparison, where no experimental factors or stimulus are introduced.

cross-pollination The transfer of pollen from the anther (male structure) of one plant to the stigma (female structure) of another plant.

cuticle A waxy layer on the outer surface of the epidermal layer. Protects against water loss.

deciduous Shedding leaves during a certain season.

dependent variable The variable in an experiment to be measured. For example, if testing the death rate of insects living on a plant after exposure to a pesticide; the death rate is the dependent variable and the pesticide is the independent variable.

display Refers to the entire science fair exhibit of which the backboard is a part.

experimental variable Also called the independent variable; the aspect or factor of an experiment that is manipulated or changed for comparison. For example, the amount of a fungicide needed to control a mold.

eukaryotic A cell containing internal organelles and a nucleus.

experimental group A test group that is subjected to experimental factors or stimulus for the sake of comparison with the control group. For example, a mold exposed to varying concentrations of fungicide.

flower The reproductive structure of angiosperms.

food chain A simple representation of "who eats what" in an ecosystem; represented by one-to-one relationships.

fruit A mature ovary of an angiosperm containing seeds.

frond The leaf of a fern plant.

fungus Primitive plants incapable of photosynthesis. Most are saprophytic, meaning they feed on decaying organic matter.

geotropism The growth of a plant directed by gravity.

gibberellins A group of plant growth hormones.

habitat The place where an organism lives. For example, an aquatic or terrestrial habitat.

herb A nonwoody seed plant.

herbivore A plant eater.

heterotroph Organisms that require an external source of organic chemical energy (food) to survive (as opposed to autotrophic). Also called *consumers*.

host The organism which supports the life of another organism such as a parasite; for example, some plants are hosts to gall-producing insects.

hyphae The filaments of a mold or a mushroom; in molds, the tip of the hyphae produce spores that produce the next generation.

hypothesis An educated guess, formulated after thorough research, to be shown true or false through experimentation.

infection A growth of microorganisms within a host that causes illness in the host.

inorganic matter Substances that are not alive and did not come from decomposed organisms.

journal Also called the project notebook; contains all notes on all aspects of a science fair project from start to finish.

kelp A common name for any of the macroscopic (large) brown algae.

lichen A type of fungus living in a symbiotic relation with algal cells.

macroscopic Large enough to see with the unaided eye.

metabolism The sum of the physical and biochemical reactions necessary for life.

mold A general term for many of the simple, filamentous fungi.

morphology The study of the appearance of an organism, including its shape, texture and color.

mycelium The main body of a multi-cellular fungi.

nut A dry, hard fruit containing a single seed.

observations A form of qualitative data collection.

organelle A membrane-enclosed structure within a cell in eukaryotic organisms.

organic Substances that compose living or dead, decaying organisms and their waste products. Carbon is the primary element.

paleobotany The study of fossilized plants.

parasite An organism that lives in or on one or more organisms (hosts) during a portion of its life. The host is not usually killed in the process.

pathogens Organisms that cause disease in other organisms.

phloem Food-conducting tissue in vascular plants.

photosynthesis The process by which light energy is converted into chemical energy. The chemical energy is in the form of carbohydrates derived from carbon dioxide in the air. The light is captured by a pigment called *chlorophyll*.

pigment A substance that absorbs light, sometimes selectively. Chlorophyll, which captures light energy during photosynthesis, is a pigment.

plankton Microscopic aquatic organisms found in most bodies of water. Plant-like plankton are called phytoplankton and animal-like plankton are called zooplankton.

pollen The male gamete (reproductive cell) of seed plants.

producer An organism that makes its own chemical energy (food), usually using energy from the sun.

protists Members of a kingdom of living things, composed of single-celled eukaryotes that do not have a cell wall. Some have chlorophyll while others do not.

qualitative studies Experimentation where data collection involves observations but no numerical results.

quantitative studies Experimentation where data collection involves measurements and numerical results.

raw data Any data collected during the course of an experiment that has not been manipulated in any way.

research Also called a literature search; locating and studying as much of the existing information about a subject as possible.

resolving power, microscope The smallest distance between two objects in which the two objects can still be distinguished from one another. If the two objects are beyond the resolving power of a microscope, the two objects appear as one.

root The part of a plant that usually descends beneath the soil or water line to anchor the plant and to absorb water and minerals.

scientific method The basic methodology of all scientific experimentation, which includes: 1) the statement of the problem to be solved or question to be answered to further science, 2) the formulation of a hypothesis, and 3) performing experimentation to determine if the hypothesis is true or false. Experimentation includes data collection, analysis, and arriving at a conclusion.

seed The mature reproductive structure (embryo) that forms after fertilization.

shoot The above-ground portion of a vascular plant, consisting of stems and leaves.

species Organisms with the potential to breed and produce viable offspring.

spore An asexual reproductive structure. Found in primitive plants.

statistics A method for analyzing numerical data.

stimulus An event that prompts a reaction or a response.

stomata Microscopic openings on the surface of leaves and stems of plants that allow gases to pass through. They are closed by bordering guard cells.

variables A factor that is changed to test the hypothesis.

weed Any plant growing where people don't want it to grow.

xylem Vascular (tubular) tissue that conducts water and minerals throughout a plant.

Sources

Scientific supply houses

You can order equipment, supplies, and live specimens for projects in this book from the companies listed in this section.

Ward's Natural Science Establishment, Inc.
5100 West Henrietta Road
Rochester, NY 14692
(800) 962-2660

or

815 Fero Lane
P.O. Box 5010
San Luis Obispo, CA 93403
(800) 872-7289

Blue Spruce Biological Supply Company
221 South Street
Castle Rock, CO 80104
(800) 621-8385

The Carolina Biological Supply Company
2700 York Road
Burlington, NC 27215
Eastern US (800) 334-5551; Western US (800) 547-1733

Connecticut Valley Biological
82 Valley Road
P.O. Box 326
Southampton, MA 01073

Fisher Scientific
4901 W. LeMoyne Street
Chicago, IL 60651
800-955-1177

Frey Scientific Company
905 Hickory Lane
P.O. Box 8101
Mansfield, OH 44901
(800) 225-FREY

Nasco
901 Janesville Avenue
P.O. Box 901
Fort Atkinson, WI 53538
(800) 558-9595

Nebraska Scientific
3823 Leavenworth Street
Omaha, NE 68105
(800) 228-7117

Powell Laboratories Division
19355 McLoughlin Boulevard
Gladstone, OR 97027
(800) 547-1733

Sargent-Welch Scientific Company
P.O. Box 1026
Skokie, IL 60076

Southern Biological Supply Company
P.O. Box 368
McKenzie, TN 38201
(800) 748-8735

Books about botany and science fairs

For more information about the science of botany and field botany, consider:

Imes, Rick. 1990. *The Practical Botanist.* New York: Simon and Schuster/Fireside.
Prescott, G.W., 1978. *How to Know the Freshwater Algae.* 3rd ed. Dubuque, Iowa: Wm. C. Brown Co. Publ.
Reid, George. 1967. *Pond Life, A Golden Guide.* New York: Golden Press.

If you are new to science fairs, here are a few good books to read. They cover all aspects of entering a science fair.

Bombaugh, Ruth. 1990. *Science Fair Success.* Hillside, NJ: Enslow Publishers.
Irtz, Maxine. 1987. *Science Fair—Developing a Successful and Fun Project.* Blue Ridge Summit, PA: TAB Books.

Tocci, Salvatore. 1986. *How To Do A Science Fair Project.* New York: Franklin Watts.

The following books can be used for additional science fair project ideas. Although most are not specifically about botany, many involve plants or can be adapted to create projects about plants.

Bochinski, Julianne, 1991. *The Complete Handbook of Science Fair Projects.* New York: Wiley & Sons, Inc.

Bonnet, Robert and Daniel Keen. 1989. *Botany: 49 Science Fair Projects.* Blue Ridge Summit, PA: Tab Books/McGraw-Hill.

Dashefsky, H. Steven, 1994. *Environmental Science: High School Science Fair Experiments.* Blue Ridge Summit, PA: TAB Books/McGraw-Hill.

Gardner, Robert, 1989. *More Ideas for Science Fair Projects.* New York: Franklin Watts.

Irtz, Maxine, 1991. *Blue-Ribbon Science Fair Projects.* Blue Ridge Summit, PA: TAB Books/McGraw-Hill.

Witherspoon, James D., 1993. *From Field to Lab, 200 Life Science Experiments for the Amateur Biologist.* Blue Ridge Summit, PA: TAB Books/McGraw-Hill.

VanCleave, Janice, 1993. *A+ Projects in Biology.* New York: John Wiley & Sons, Inc.

VanCleave, Janice, 1990. *Biology for Every Kid: 101 Easy Experiments that Really Work.* New York: John Wiley & Sons, Inc.

For information about the International Science and Engineering Fairs and valuable information about Adult Sponsorship, write to: The Science Service at 1719 N Street, N.W., Washington, DC 20036; or call them at (202) 785-2255.

If you are interested in joining an organization dedicated to studying and preserving plant life, contact any of these groups:

The American Horticultural Society
P.O. Box 0105
Mt. Vernon, VA 22301

The Garden Club of America
598 Madison Avenue
New York, NY 10461

National Arbor Day Foundation
100 Arbor Avenue
Nebraska City, NE 68410

National Wildflower Research Center
2600 FM 973 North
Austin, TX 78725

Canadian Wildflower Society
35 Bauer Crescent
Unionville, Ontario L3R4H3
CANADA

Index

Boldface numbers indicate illustrations.

About the author

H. Steven Dashefsky is an adjunct professor of environmental science at Marymount College in Tarrytown, New York. He is the founder of the Center for Environmental Literacy, which was created to educate the public about environmental problems and solutions. He holds a B.S. in biology and an M.S. in entomology and is the author of more than 10 books that simplify science and technology.